𝔓erfect 𝔓artners™

Should You Stay or Should You Leave?
Step-By-Step

Books by
Carolyn & Wes Huff

Perfect Partners™
Make Your Hopes & Dreams for a Great Marriage Come True

Perfect Partners™
Find Your Perfect Partner Step-By-Step

Perfect Partners™
When You Think You've Found Your Perfect Partner Step-By-Step

Perfect Partners™
Should You Stay or Should You Leave? Step-By-Step

Perfect Partners™
Should You Stay or Should You Leave?
Step-By-Step

Patent Pending

Workbook Companion to

Perfect Partners™
Make Your Hopes and Dreams for a Great Marriage Come True

Carolyn & Wes Huff

Empowerment Solutions, Inc.,
Severna Park, Maryland 21146

Printed in the United States of America

For information address:

Empowerment Solutions, Inc.
550 M Ritchie Highway
Suite 142
Severna Park, MD 21146

Library of Congress Cataloging-in-Publication Data

Huff, Carolyn & Wes Huff
Perfect Partners™: Should You Stay or Should You Leave? Step-By-Step / Carolyn & Wes Huff

ISBN 1-891336-03-7 $18.95 (paperback)
Library of Congress Catalog Card Number: 97-94580

Cover Designed by Cherry Hepburn, Putnam & Smith, 12309 Moorpark St., Suite #3, Studio City, CA 91604, (818) 505-1104
Book printed and bound by BookCrafters, Chelsea, MI 48118
Distribution by BookMasters Inc., Mansfield, OH 44905

10 9 8 7 6 5 4 3 2 1
FIRST EDITION

Dedication

To God: It has been our mission to bring your love into this world. Thank you for allowing us to succeed in our way.

To Ryan & Amanda: You showed us that great marriages are humanly possible.

To Jeff & Tracey and Todd & Alysa: You wanted a great marriage and got it, too.

To Jennie: We love you and wish you the best.

To David: You're on your way. You can have it all if you want it.

To Wes, From Carolyn: You made it possible for me. Loving you is easy. Loving you is a gift to me.

To Carolyn, From Wes: You are the one I've been looking for all of my life.

To Carolyn's patients: Thank you. Sharing in your lives was a gift to me.

To Stella: Your belief in me came at a turning point in my life. Thank you for being my teacher in the truest sense of the word. I'll never forget what you did for me. Love, Carolyn

To our teachers who missed the mark: Your lives would change for the better if you only realized that you are the student.

To all that thought you were our student, you were really our teacher. And to all that thought you were our teacher, you were really our student.

Thank you from the bottom of our hearts. We wish you the love of your life.

Carolyn & Wes

Table of Contents

Dear Reader | 9

Part I: Should You Stay or Should You Leave? | 15

We've Been Where You Are | 17

The Land Mines of a Troubled Marriage | 18

Have You Married the Wrong Person? | 21

Deciding Whether to Stay or Leave | 22

Decide What Kind of a Marriage You Want | 23

Poor Marriages | 24

Marriages of Convenience | 25

It's a Myth that All Marriages are Lots of Hard Work | 26

Don't Tie Up All of Your Time and Energy in the Wrong Marriage | 27

A Great Marriage Gives You | 28

Let's Add to the Equation a Bit of Mysticism | 29

What Does This All Mean? | 30

Challenge the Myth: You Can Have A Great Marriage if You Know What to Do | 31

Avoid Being Dishonest With Yourself About the Way Things Are | 32

Is This Your Perfect Partner Disguised Behind Poor Relationship Skills or Not? | 35

Five Crucial Questions | 35

Your Perfect Partner | 36

16 Differences That Make a Difference | 37

Begin By Asking Yourself the Five Crucial Questions | 41

Question 1: 16 Differences That Make a Difference - Do You Match? | 42

Score Yourself on the 16 Differences | 115

Now What? | 120

Question 2: How effective is your partner? | 121

Question 3: Does your partner have his or her head straight? | 133

Question 4: Is your partner genuine, honest, and trustworthy? Do they have character and

integrity? | 144
Question 5: Is there some magic? Are you
attracted to each other? | 155

Part II: Sometimes Leaving Can Be Love | 187
When the Best Thing to Do is to Leave | 189
Rejection | 191
Unfinished Business | 198

Part III: Have a Great Marriage | 201
When you Know the Best for Everyone is to Stay | 203
Are You in a Long-term Relationship, but not
Married? | 210
Great Sex | 210
A Word about Quickies | 218
Boundaries | 218
The First Task of Every Marriage | 219
Personal Boundaries | 220
Couple Boundaries | 220
Special Boundaries - Rituals, Ceremonies,
and Symbols | 226
Book & Consultation Order Form | 235

June 30, 1997

Dear Reader,

Thank you for your interest in our ideas about love and marriage. If you are reading this introduction, you are most likely, having some difficulty in your relationship or marriage. Nothing is lonelier than a troubled marriage. Nothing is more traumatic than the emotional suffering of a husband and wife and their children as a result of a troubled marriage.

Until now, nothing like this workbook has existed. Until now, many therapists have resisted the temptation to tell couples whether to leave or stay in their marriages. In their attempt to stay neutral and not foist their opinions on others, a valuable opportunity has been lost to help people understand how to make such a difficult decision. When such a time comes in someone's life, objective information and role modeling can be invaluable as a resource to others. That is what this workbook has been designed to do. Give you objective information to assist you in thinking for yourself and, while listening to and considering your feelings, help you to rely on your intellect to make a clear decision. Ambivalence — not being in the marriage and not being out of the marriage — is extremely harmful to you, to your partner, and to the life of your family. We want you to be clear about whether to stay or to leave. And then really commit yourself to your decision.

We are adamantly and unabashedly for marriage. We believe so strongly in marriage that we believe we must share the knowledge we've gained through our own unhappy experiences in marriages to the wrong partner. The unhappiness Carolyn's patients have brought into therapy through the years reinforces both our understanding of what goes wrong, but also how to fix what's wrong. Most importantly, we want to share with you what a great marriage is all about. A great marriage is what we found with each other and it is so different from any other relationship we've ever had that we feel compelled to share what we've learned.

We are so against divorce that we've gone to great lengths to articulate to as many people as possible what we've learned that can prevent divorce — before they get into trouble.

Unfortunately, if you're reading this book, unless you're just curious, you didn't have the opportunity to learn what we know in time to prevent an attachment to the wrong partner. Or maybe your problems come from inadequate relationship skills. Now you must decide whether to cut your losses and leave, or master better relationship skills and stay.

We have designed this workbook for couples in troubled relationships and troubled marriages.

First, this workbook will help you decide whether your difficulties stem from incompatibility on differences that make a difference and/or from poor relationship skills. Most of what's been written and available to couples is oriented toward the idea that any marriage to someone good enough can be fixed if you only know how to communicate and solve conflict. If you will only learn a few recipes, you can repair your broken marriage. We disagree. Only some marital problems are related to inadequate relationship skills. When your differences cause a threat to your integrity you cannot compromise or negotiate without losing yourself in the marriage. And differences that make a difference — basic values you hold and appreciate about life — are not gender related. If you believe that men are from Mars and women are from Venus, you must be from Jupiter. You can create a peaceful coexistence by practicing healthy relationship skills, but you cannot ever have a great marriage with someone that challenges your integrity.

After you've determined whether your problems are differences that make a difference and/or poor relationship skills we'll guide you through your decision making process about the outcomes of your choices. In the event that you're with the wrong partner, we'll help you to leave gracefully, knowing that only by leaving will you free yourself and your partner for marriage to your perfect partner and a great marriage. Only by having a great marriage can you role model one for your children. If you're already with your perfect partner, we'll help you polish your relationship skills and nudge your personal growth so you can have a great marriage.

We each married partners, initially, with whom we didn't match. We had unhappy marriages to varying degrees for many years. We lived through the torment of our unhappiness, the unhappiness of our spouse, and our children's unhappiness for years. Some of the fallout from all of that unhappiness is still with us today. You have something in this book that we didn't have. It is our hope that being with you through our book, through what must be some of your darkest hours, will give you the companionship, insight, knowledge, and courage to do what's best for you and your family.

We had to make the decisions you have to make and it isn't easy. But the outcome of doing so will mean more to your life than you can even imagine. The result of our own painful decisions to leave poor marriages is better than we ever imagined. Our marriage isn't like any other relationship we've ever had. We had no idea that marriage could be so good. With some heartfelt work, you can have a great marriage, too.

One of the most interesting outcomes of making our ideas about love, relationships, and marriage public has been the resistance we've encountered to reconsidering notions that have been etched into our brains. If you find yourself resisting our ideas, keep reading. Give yourself a chance to ponder their meanings over time. Open your mind to a new way of understanding and thinking about love. After you've allowed yourself to try the ideas on for size over a period of time you can always go back to thinking what you've always thought before. We'll wager a bet that you won't. Because, after you've really tried this all on and lived with it for a while, you'll know it makes sense. Give yourself a chance to really think about it all – resist your resistance. We believe you'll be thankful you did.

Another fascinating outcome of going public has been our being challenged with what we think is jealousy. If you find yourself feeling jealous and then defending those feelings with ridicule, stop. You can have this, too. Don't be jealous. Get it for yourself. You have everything to gain and nothing to lose except misery. Don't you deserve to be happy?

You have chosen to challenge the norm and we wish
you all of the best.

Highest regards,
Carolyn & Wes Huff
http://www.perfectpartners.net

Part 1

Should You Stay or Should You Leave?

We've Been Where You Are

Let us begin by telling you that we have suffered the turmoil and pain of poor marriages that you find yourself having. We both agonized over whether to stay or to leave. We both tried everything we knew how to fix our troubled marriages. We suffered deeply over ending our marriages to the wrong partner. We both stayed too long.

We have learned this from the inside out.

In many ways, divorce is far more painful than death. Divorce is always painful and difficult, even when friendly. So painful and difficult that we believe that the attitude that, "there's always divorce" as an escape hatch, does serious disservice to you and your partner. But sometimes the pain of staying is far greater and does enormous damage to each partner and especially the children.

We believe adamantly that children need two competent parents and a stable family for healthy growth and development. But leaving some marriage circumstances is far healthier for children than staying.

With the destruction of our families over the last couple of decades there has been some discussion of making divorce harder to get – to reverting to a past where people were trapped in miserable lives. We believe that peoples' lives are far too important to do that, but we agree that something must be done to help our families thrive and raise competent and happy children to adulthood. Something must be done to help us become all that we can become.

It is because we believe in marriage so strongly and believe that divorce is miserably destructive that we came to the conclusion that we had to help find a better solution. When we found each other and experienced a relationship like none we'd ever had before, we said, "this is the answer." We must let others know what's possible. Finding and marrying the right partner – your perfect partner – is the answer to strengthening marriage and preventing divorce.

We have decided that we must take personal responsibility to begin the process of slowly chipping away at the defensive attitudes that we've developed about love, relationships, and marriage.

We're sad to meet you this way, but we're deeply happy that you've decided to meet your problem head-on. We'll do whatever we can to help you end your ambivalence and start on a path of commitment to the best interests of you, your mate, and your families. Thank you for giving us the opportunity to help.

The Land Mines of a Troubled Marriage

You may or may not realize all of the miserable things that can happen when you marry the wrong partner. Since you're in a troubled marriage right now, the chances are that you've already experienced some of these destructive results, but we want to make absolutely certain that you realize the negative things are related to the bad marriage. Some of the destructive results of marriage to the wrong partner are:

- -Stress-related illness
- -Emotional turmoil, including loss of
  trust in the opposite sex, resent
  ment, bitterness, and hatred
- -Assault & battery
- -Increased poor self-esteem
- -Diminished self-confidence
- -Work problems
- -Financial Problems
- -Addiction
- -Children's distress

The children of troubled marriages suffer from sibling jealousy, insecurity, nightmares, school difficulties, drug use, and later, poor relationships of their own.

What puts a marriage on the divorce block? Mainly, it's exhaustion and pain from the constant strain of managing differences. Differences that threaten the integrity of either partner intensify the need to fight to the finish – and rightly so. The degree of difference, as well as, the methods a couple uses to manage their differences, spells out making it or not. And making it can be in a matter of degrees from peaceful coexistence and parallel play to an energized, great marriage, with a vitality that fuels itself.

The Ladies' Home Journal has featured a column about marriage for fifty years called Can This Marriage Be Saved? It's billed the "most popular, most enduring Women's Magazine feature in the world." The book written by the producers of that column – Can This Marriage Be Saved? (Workman, 1994) – identifies seven underlying areas causing marital distress, that remain fundamentally the same from generation to generation, no matter what the specifics are from marriage to marriage. These tasks are all skills that help or hinder managing differences. These seven tasks of marriage are basically relationship skills or skills of daily living. The column directs its efforts to mending broken relationships by improving relationship skills, which is what most books and therapists do with problem marriages. It makes sense to improve everything that it's possible to improve to make the best of what you have. But doing so only improves poor marriages and gets you a marriage of convenience unless you have an underlying compatibility on differences that make a difference. Perfecting your relationship skills still may not get you a great marriage and a great marriage is what everyone deserves.

Identified by The Ladies' Home Journal as the most frequent causes of marital distress are:

> -Lack of Trust
> -Poor Communication
> -Poor Management of Anger
> -Power Struggles
> -Poor Money Management
> -Problems with Sexual Intimacy
> -Outside Pressures from Work,
> Family, and Friends

We Would Add
> -Differences That Make a Difference
> Resulting in Endless Negotiation
> and Challenge to Your or Your Partner's Integrity

Have You Married the Wrong Person?

Most people depend on a romantic accident to find their mate. The criteria they use to know if they've found the right person is physical chemistry. "If we feel attracted, we must be right for each other," is what most people think.

The major reason marriages fail is that you select the wrong marriage partner. People marry the wrong person for a number of reasons. Following is a list of reasons that people marry the wrong partner. How many apply to you?

- -You didn't realize how important it is to match on the 16 differences that make a difference.
- -You believed that mismatches are natural. Men are from Mars and Women are from Venus, as John Grey would say.
- -You believed that you would find your perfect partner through a romantic accident- thus leaving the most important decision of your life to chance.
- -You surrendered to the prince and princess fantasy. Your prince was rescuing you or you were rescuing your princess.
- -Your partner oversold himself or herself during courtship – only to reveal their true self later.
- -You minimized the bad characteristics of the person you were in "love" with.
- -You failed to realize that falling in love is a choice.
- -Physical chemistry overcame all sensibility.

-Familiarity – you were attracted to
someone who is like one of your parents.
-Limited choices – You settled for the best
that you thought you could get in a
competitive dating marketplace.
-You were seeking approval from others.
-You didn't know yourself so you didn't
know how well you matched with your
partner.
-You didn't realize how bad marriage to the
wrong partner can be, and how painful
breaking up is.
-You assumed that you could easily get a
divorce.

If one reason applies to you, the chances are that you've married the wrong person. If more than one reason applies, the chances are stronger that you married the wrong person.

We designed the exercises that follow to help you to validate that you've married the wrong person or that you've married the right person and you just can't tell because of poor relationship skills and issues haunting you or your mate from the past.

Deciding Whether to Stay or Leave

The key element to making the right decision about whether to stay or leave is deciding whether your marriage is suffering from poor relationship skills or from incompatibility on the 16 differences that make a difference. This workbook is designed to help you make the distinction.

Decide What Kind of a Marriage You Want

First, we want you to consider what kind of marriage you want. Without your goal in mind it will be more difficult to see where you're going and impossible to hit the target. Remember: begin with the end in mind (Covey, 1989).

Most people would probably call most marriages good or bad. We want to more carefully define the kinds of marriages we see and the kind we've come to know ourselves. In defining the types of marriages more carefully, we realize that we've made some arbitrary decisions about what labels to give the kinds of marriages we can identify. You can hair-split and argue that our definitions aren't quite right – we had a few discussions ourselves, but we think we're reasonably close to good working definitions.

Three kinds of marriages exist:

1. Poor marriages
2. Marriages of convenience
3. Great Marriages

You can argue that a fourth, a good marriage, exists and maybe it does, but we want people to start realizing that what they've called good in the past is more often a marriage of convenience. We'll concede that marriages exist that are somewhere between a marriage of convenience and a great marriage, but we want the differences to contrast to a greater degree so you can be sure about exactly what a great marriage offers above all of the others.

Poor Marriages

We define a poor marriage as any marriage that has some kind of abuse going on. The abuse may be in the form of physical battering, emotional, mental, and/or verbal abuse. In a poor marriage, one or both partners attack the other in such a way as to diminish self-esteem and self-confidence. Physical attacks may cause physical injury. Partners in a poor marriage attempt to control each other rather than relating to each other out of respect. Partners in poor marriages generally are without the capacity to operate in the world as competent adults. They may perform adequately in other areas of their life, but personal relationships – in particular, marriage – tap into dependency issues, incompetence in handling many tasks of daily living, and render the person incapable of having a satisfying relationship.

Problems in poor marriages usually consist of a combination of both incompatibility and poor relationship skills. Dependency is the big issue. For it is dependency that keeps you in any situation that can harm you. And it is dependency that drives the abuser to controlling their partner's behavior so they will be taken care of. Yes, the bully is dependent. And bullying is designed to get their needs met.

A poor marriage not only deprives you of an opportunity to have the benefits of a great marriage, but it can harm you physically, emotionally, and mentally. Poor marriages cripple you, your mate, and your children.

Marriages of Convenience

A marriage of convenience is a marriage between partners with parallel lives. Partners in a marriage of convenience have learned to peacefully coexist. A marriage of convenience is between partners that have little in common – incompatibility of many values or interests – but have reasonable relationship skills that allow them to navigate marriage without much conflict. A marriage of convenience doesn't actively and directly harm partners, but passively withholds the energizing nurturance and validation that a great marriage offers.

Unfortunately, a marriage of convenience has a low level of intimacy. And the level of intimacy is what differentiates marriage from other friendships. Having a partner in whom you can confide and disclose yourself – with whom you can be intimate – can save your life, literally (read Dr. James Lynch's The Broken Heart).

Marriages of convenience will not cause you to wither on the vine, but they never add fertilizer to help you become the best you can be.

Many people settle for a marriage of convenience – especially at the relief of improving their marriage from a poor marriage. Some don't realize anything more is possible. Many people think that marriages of convenience are good marriages just because there's an absence of conflict. It isn't true. And even though it may sometimes make sense to settle for less than the best, it's still possible to have more.

It's a Myth that All Marriages are Lots of Hard Work

Only marriages to the wrong partner are endless compromise and negotiation, leaving you little time and energy for anything in your life but making your marriage work.

Theoretically, it's possible to turn a poor marriage into a great marriage if not too much damage is done before the partners heal themselves and learn good relationship skills. Unfortunately, the pain and suffering caused by any form of abuse erodes trust and friendliness rapidly. And the kind of life circumstances that cause someone to become an adult who uses abusive control and manipulation takes time and determination to repair. It can be done, but can it be done before too much harm is done? Once you've hurt the other person or they've hurt you past the point of no return, even if you grow and mature, you'll most likely have lost the opportunity to continue the relationship. How do you find friendship and warmth under so many layers of resentment and hostility?

And if you lack compatibility on the 16 differences that make a difference, you can never make it to a great marriage from a poor marriage, but only to a marriage of convenience at best.

Partners in a marriage of convenience may have good relationship skills. (If they've achieved peace by avoidance then they don't have good relationship skills – they're just good at avoidance.) Partners in a marriage of convenience don't beat each other up physically or mentally. The harm partners do to each other are harms of omission. Their problem is a lack of compatibility on the 16 differences that make a difference. You can't turn a marriage of convenience into a great marriage because of the absence of compatibility on differences that threaten your integrity. A great psychologist, Erik Erikson, identified eight stages of psychological development from birth to death. The last stage is integrity versus despair. Despair is what you get when you sell yourself out. Given that, what do you think will happen to you when you reach that stage of your life and development – the stage of integrity versus despair – when you've bargained and compromised away your integrity even half of the time? Some differences don't make much difference, but the 16 differences that make a difference matter more than you can imagine.

The saddest part of poor marriages and marriages of convenience is that it doesn't have to be that way.

Don't Tie Up All of Your Time and Energy in the Wrong Marriage

A great marriage is composed of intimacy, active interest in your partner's life, good relationship skills, and great sex. A great marriage is positively energizing.

In a great marriage partners have a high level of compatibility on each of 16 differences that make a difference. That high level of compatibility, in turn, offers each partner emotional safety, respect, and friendship. Such natural approval, admiration, and validation foster a high level of satisfaction with your life and the synergy created boosts you to top performance and engagement in life. Differences of opinion are a minor part of life and are managed respectfully. Both partners win all of the time. Partners in a great marriage handle the tasks of daily living smoothly and easily. Partners in a great marriage know how to set healthy limits for their children and provide the best possible environment for children to learn how to pick the right marriage partner and how to have a great marriage.

A great marriage is fun. A great marriage works of its own accord. Gone forever is the need to work hard to make it work.

A Great Marriage Gives You

A great marriage:

-   Prevents all of the land mines of a poor marriage or a marriage of convenience
-   Liberates time and energy for life's tasks, and provides a platform from which to meet other challenges your life brings
-   Offers you the chance to be the best you can be at work, play, and relationships
-   Contributes to physical and mental health

-Balances the work of life with fun and
   recreation
-Gives you energy
-Contributes to a variety of successes
-Provides an opportunity for your children
   to see healthy role models for marriage
   and life
-Contributes to the health of your
   community

Let's Add to the Equation a Bit of Mysticism

For those of you who haven't worked through our first workbook, Find Your Perfect Partner Step-By-Step, consider this. Suppose for a minute, that Earth is indeed, a school for souls – for spirits to evolve. And on Earth we have male and female humans. Carolyn believes that reincarnation allows us to evolve over many lifetimes. She also believes that marriage is an opportunity to internalize the opposite sex's so-called male or female qualities. Our objective as human students is to individuate and become who we are and live honestly who we are, rather than fused in a group of like-mindedness.

Carolyn believes that, one of the tasks male and female humans need to accomplish is to become complete within ourselves. We're here to develop both male and female aspects within each of us, male attributes being action-oriented and female attributes being receptive, more passive, and contemplative. We're most competent when we can rely on the reception of ideas, introspection, and then act accordingly.

Marriage offers us the opportunity to learn from each other and helps us evolve. Male attributes are no better than female and vice versa. Both need to be part of each of us. When two marriage partners are complete within themselves, when they each can handle tasks of daily living competently and live to their highest potential, they can be free to stay in a loving marriage without any need to control the other. With the incorporation of male and female traits, we can be interdependent in our marriages rather than dependent, co-dependent, or independent (parallel lives).

If this hypothesis is true, having a great marriage becomes a necessity, eventually. Yes, marriages to partners that are very different from us offers a set of circumstances that help us grow or can demoralize and defeat us. Yes, marriages to partners different from us can teach us many things. At what cost? Eventually, as you evolve, life's lessons must shift to becoming more positively and completely who you are, not spending your time and energy on what's wrong and doesn't work.

What Does This All Mean?

A great marriage is important to you for many reasons.

Great marriages exist in a climate of emotional safety, respect, admiration, friendship, affection, and support.

Challenge the Myth: You Can Have A Great Marriage if You Know What To Do

No one can tell you what to do. Whether to stay or leave must be your decision. But we hope that given some new information, we can help you make this very difficult conclusion – whichever way it may go.

You deserve a great marriage. Learn whether you have the makings right now and make it so or leave and make it possible for you and your partner to find a perfect partner and have a great marriage.

Unfortunately, not very many great marriages exist. You don't have many role models to watch.

When we discovered how different and wonderful a great marriage is when we found each other, we decided we had to tell others how to find their own perfect partners. A great marriage is even better than we ever dreamed.

Avoid Being Dishonest With Yourself About The Way Things Are

In order for you to make this decision, you'll need to use all of the courage, emotional health, and self-honesty you have.

We have a tendency to minimize other people's character flaws or differences when we find them attractive. When you've built a history together, it can be even easier to make excuses. And, of course, once you've made a commitment to someone, most of us hold the value of keeping that commitment. The question is where to draw the line? When does keeping the commitment help us and when does it do damage?

The term in psychology for this is idealization. Idealizing someone means that you're pushing their best points to the foreground and their bad points to the background. In the case of evaluating your marriage or relationship, it means pushing its problems to the background and denying the real damage being done. Or, conversely, making a too hasty retreat and taking the easy way out.

When you focus your attention on what's good, postponing an honest look at the real, whole person or relationship, you only postpone your grief. And you diminish your self-esteem by not handling the problem more realistically.

Idealizing begins in childhood when we're so dependent, and are at the mercy of our caretakers for our lives. We need to believe that the adults taking care of us know how to do anything that needs to be done. What in the world would happen to us if they didn't know how to take care of us? We're little and helpless in the beginning and see our parents (and other adults) as perfect and all knowing. We idealize them.

At some point in our childhood or later, we suddenly realize that our parents and other adults are just humans, with ordinary amounts of knowledge and skills. It's usually a shock to discover they're just like other common people. In other words, they're not infallible. This discovery is part of our growing up. If we continue to idealize others, we don't develop a realistic picture of the world and operate under the assumption that the idealized picture we have is the truth.

Part of maturity is developing a realistic picture of others and of ourselves. By being competent, we become less dependent on others to be perfect. This helps us see them as they are.

To end your ambivalence you must evaluate your marriage and your partner, realistically. Avoid pushing their undesirable characteristics and their differences to the background. This is difficult to do if you're needy, lonely, and dependent. It's difficult to do if there's a strong physical attraction between the two of you. You must use all of your mental/emotional muscle to be realistic, and to be able to end a relationship with someone who isn't right for you.

One further caution! One characteristic of abusive, self-centered people who would take advantage of you (and worse) is their charm! One of the ways people get away with not maturing and being abusive is their charm. Abuse is a drastic form of manipulation to get what you want. The combination of your idealizing someone and their charming ways is particularly deadly when it comes to relationships. The best way to avoid any kind of abusive relationship, from the mildest to the most abusive, is to get your head straight. Work your own issues through, be competent to handle tasks of daily living, trust your perceptions, and have the ability to see the world as it is, not as you wish it were!

In our workbooks written to help singles find and know their perfect partner, we say, by pushing undesirable characteristics to the background and ignoring them, you're only postponing disappointment and misery! Later, when it's impossible to ignore or make excuses for these characteristics any longer, you'll be that much more attached to the relationship, will have more of an investment, and may even have children. It's much better for you to face up to reality right now! In most cases, the wrong marriage is far worse than no marriage.

Is that where you are?

Lest we scare you unnecessarily, we want to acknowledge that there's a time and a place for charm, which enhances behaviors that are considerate and mature. Charm isn't necessarily bad. It depends on how the person uses charm. The kind of charm that's warm and adds to the pleasure between two respectful, considerate, loving, nurturing, and supportive adults is wonderful. It's a skill that will add to your relationship; charm adds to falling in love when the time comes! Just don't confuse this wonderful kind of charm with the charm that someone uses to manipulate you to get his or her way. Be honest with yourself and see right though it.

Is This Your Perfect Partner Disguised Behind Poor Relationship Skills or Not?

This workbook is designed to help you decide whether you've found your perfect partner for a great marriage and just need help with your relationship skills or whether you've married the wrong partner and can never have the chance for a great marriage.

Five Crucial Questions

We've distilled a highly specific list of 16 differences that make a difference, which, when carefully matched to your mate will prevent the first cause of marital failure – incompatibility.

We added four questions to the measure of compatibility concerning your partner's level of function and your attraction to each other. These five questions, when answered as honestly as possible, can tell you clearly whether you've found your perfect partner for your own great marriage.

The difference in answers between question one – how well do you match on the 16 differences that make a difference – and the remaining four questions will help you differentiate between incompatibility and poor relationship skills.

First we'll describe the 16 differences that make a difference for those of you who are learning about them for the first time. Following the 16 differences we'll provide you with an exercise and guidance to take a look at what you have in your relationship. We'll use the example of two couples throughout the workbook to enliven the exercises and their interpretations.

Your Perfect Partner

You and your perfect partner must have similar world views. Take a moment here and think about this. Over the years we've learned that respecting others' differences adds a positive dimension to our culture. America has long been known for its melting pot and, as citizens, we take pride in opening our minds and hearts to all kinds of people. As long as another person's beliefs, attitudes, and practices don't harm someone else we say every one has the right to believe and do, as they want.

When we have differences with a friend, neighbor, or coworker we can go our separate ways and control the amount of exposure to them. Distance makes respecting differences relatively easy to do.

Marriage intensifies differences because of proximity and raising children.

Some differences don't matter as much as others. If you like to drink milk and someone else only likes iced tea, it doesn't matter much.

Some differences make a difference. These 16 differences really make a difference. When you marry someone with much of a difference in even one of the differences on our list, you'll seriously jeopardize your chances for a great marriage. Marrying someone with differences in these core values will call your or your partner's integrity into question with every compromise and negotiation. Differences in these core values necessitate winners and losers in conflict. But marriage must create wins for both partners. If one partner loses in a marriage, both lose.

Your perfect partner is someone who shares core values with you. Your differences don't interfere with integrity. Differences of opinion don't call for a winner and a loser. Children don't have to pick loyalties in order to model their parents. Marriage partners easily have admiration, respect, validation, and support for a partner with similar values. Compromise and negotiation doesn't hurt someone every time. Compromise and negotiation take a minor role in day-to-day living.

Perfect Partners™ have a chance to build up tremendous amounts of positive feelings for each other.

16 Differences That Make a Difference

1. Sex drives/sexual interests/demonstration of affection – How often do you like to have sex? How important is sex to you? How do you express your sexuality? Do you like to hold hands? Are you comfortable kissing in public or in front of the kids? How adventuresome are your sexual interests? What are your beliefs and practices about issues of birth control and safe sex?

2. Age – What is your age?

3. Health and fitness, including the habits of smoking, drinking, or using drugs – What do you believe and practice in regard to taking care of yourself – your health and fitness? What is your diet? What is your exercise routine? Do you smoke? Do you drink alcohol? Do you use drugs? What do you think about those issues? How do you think health and fitness issues affect children?

4. Where to live – Where do you want to live? Do you have allergies or other health reasons for living in certain areas? How flexible are you about where you want to live? Will your career influence where you live? What climates are most conducive to your well being? Do you enjoy leisure activities that require proximity to certain climates or terrain? Does it matter how close you live to your extended family?

5. Education/Intelligence – To what level of education do you aspire? What are your beliefs about education and intelligence? What are your intellectual interests? What do you like to talk about? What topics spark your curiosity?

6. Lifestyle (Formal versus Informal; active versus passive) – Do you like to take off your shoes and put your feet up? Do you like everything in its place or is your home a place to let your hair down? Would you rather entertain at a backyard barbecue or a dinner party? Are you child and family oriented or career and philanthropically oriented? Do you enjoy activities requiring passivity or would you rather be physically active? How do you balance formal and informal aspects of your life? How do you balance activity and passivity?

7. Views about work/Level of ambition – What are your career ambitions? What work do you do or what work would you like to do? What hours do you work? What would be the ideal balance of work and play to you? What kind of an income will it take to support the lifestyle you desire?

8. Views on how to handle and spend money – How do you want to spend, save, and invest? What are your short- and long-term financial goals?

What meanings do you attach to money?

9. Expectations of marriage – How much time do you want to spend with your partner? Do you want to be best friends or share confidences with other best friends, too? What do you believe about male and female roles in a marriage and a family? What do you expect marriage to provide for you?

10. Physical characteristics attractive to you – What about looks are important to you? What does your perfect partner look like? Are there certain body types or features that turn you on more than others? What styles of clothing do you admire?

11. Religious beliefs and practices – Religion itself isn't the issue here. Your beliefs and practices are the issue. What are your religious beliefs and practices? How do you want to raise any children in regard to religious beliefs and practices? What part does spirituality play in your life?

12. Political beliefs and practices – What are your political beliefs and practices? What part does politics play in your life?

13. Children: Having them and raising them – Do you want children? How many and when? Describe your disciplinary style. Describe parental roles. What does parenting mean to you?

14. Life stage – What is the focus of your life right now? Are you finishing school? Are you just beginning a career? Have you settled into your career? Are you raising children? Are you childless? Are you planning a career change? Are you planning for retirement?

15. Common leisure interests – What do you do for fun? How do you balance fun and work? Do you like physical activity or would you rather read or watch TV or a movie? What balance of active and passive leisure activity do you like? What kind of activity recharges your batteries and refreshes you? Do you like solitary activity or would you rather spend your leisure with others? How many others? How much time do you devote to leisure? How much money do you devote to leisure? Do you like to plan your activities ahead of time or would you rather act spontaneously?

16. Energy levels – How much energy do you have? What time of the day do you have energy? What time of the day do you crash? Are you a night person or a day person? Do you have more or less mental or physical energy? How much energy do you have to be a companion and friend? How much energy do you have to be a parent?

Begin By Asking Yourself the Five Crucial Questions

Turn to the following exercise to ask yourself five crucial questions. Be as brutally honest with yourself as you can be in answering these questions. Postponing the truth will only prolong everyone's misery.

Throughout the workbook we'll be following the progress of two couples to show you, in real life, how to implement this process. We've changed their names and identities to protect their privacy.

In some cases we have blended cases to illustrate a point, but we've essentially left their stories untouched.

Question 1: 16 Differences That Make a Difference - Do You Match?

Describe Yourself

Sex drives/sexual interests/demonstration of affection – How often do you like to have sex? How important is sex to you? How do you express your sexuality? Do you like to hold hands? Are you comfortable kissing in public or in front of the kids? How adventuresome are your sexual interests? What are your beliefs and practices about issues of birth control and safe sex?

_____

_____

_____

_____

_____

_____

_____

_____

_____

_____

_____

_____

_____

_____

Describe Your Partner

_____

_____

_____

_____

_____

_____

_____

_____

_____

_____

_____

_____

_____

_____

_____

_____

_____

_____

**Score the Match from 1 (no match)
to 10 (best match)**

Examples

Couple #1

Gary and Susan had been locked in battle for
years. They'd been to couples counseling a few
times and were never able to resolve their conflict.
Nothing they did seemed to help. This time Susan
was threatening divorce and Gary was determined
to fix their marriage.

Gary and Susan have been married for 18 years and
are in their 40's. They have one school age child
and two teenagers. Both are professionals.

As with all couples in this situation, you have to
begin at the beginning. Carolyn explained to them
that they needed more information and that the
first step was to evaluate exactly what their problems were. To know exactly what they were dealing
with they needed to know whether their conflicts
were related to incompatibility and/or poor relationship skills. So they began by answering five
crucial questions:

1. 16 differences that make a difference – Do you
   match?
2. How effective is your partner?
3. Does your partner have their head straight?
4. Is your partner genuine, honest, and trustworthy? Do they have character and integrity?
5. Is there some magic? Are you attracted to each
   other?

Take your time answering these questions.
Consider them carefully and you'll clarify what you
must do.

Gary and Susan each wrote their descriptions for

the first difference that makes a difference. Because they minimized the importance of these differences, they had to repeat this exercise weeks into their therapy. Take your time and give full consideration to how you match.

Gary's answer: I am very dissatisfied with our sex life. Susan doesn't ever want to have sex anymore. What am I supposed to do? Sometimes she lets me have sex with her, but there's nothing in it for her. She doesn't want me to satisfy or pleasure her. She just wants me to get it over with. It's terribly rejecting. I used to be fairly affectionate with her, but she blows me off so much I don't even try anymore. We used to be much better matched in the beginning.

At the very beginning of our relationship we were in college. Susan was much more interested in me than I was in her. She used to drop by and hang around more than I wanted. I had just broken up with another relationship and I wasn't ready to settle down into dating one person yet. Her hanging around was irritating to me at times. But she kept at it and at some point I decided we should get married. We'd spent some time away from each other and I missed her, so then I began to pursue her more.

Susan's answer: I can't even stand to have sex with Gary anymore. He always wants to turn it into a major production and I'm just not interested. I'm mad at him, I'm exhausted from working and the children, and I just don't care anymore. When we do have sex together, if I want to be satisfied I don't have any trouble getting satisfied and Gary knows what to do. But I just don't care anymore. Our relationship is so much work and so exhausting to me that I just want to be left alone.

Gary's score = 2
Susan's score = 5

Couple #2
Anne Marie and Matthew started this process after Matthew announced that he'd had enough and was seeking legal counsel for a divorce. Anne Marie decided that he meant business and wanted to see if they could keep their marriage together. She was distressed because, even though they were having more conflict, she loved Matthew and didn't want a divorce. She wanted to spend the rest of her life with him.

They are in their middle 30's and have two school age children. Both are business professionals.

Anne Marie's answer: I am very excited by Matthew. The first four years of our marriage were wonderful. Our courtship was wonderful. I wish we could have what we had before. I'm very attracted to Matthew except when I'm mad at him. When I get mad at him I wish he'd just leave me alone.

We have a very good sex life together. I love making love with him. At least that hasn't gone to pot since we started fighting so much. But I don't feel like making love as much anymore. Partly because we fight so much and partly because Matthew works so much, he travels, and I'm tired from my own work and the kids. It used to be much better, but sex is still good when we have it.

I like the way Matthew's so affectionate. He isn't afraid to hold my hand and be affectionate.

Matthew's answer: We have great sex, but we don't have it often enough. I'd like to have more. And Anne Marie won't let me be as affectionate as I'd like. I think it's because we fight and then she brushes me off. When we're not fighting we both like to be affectionate.

The first four years of our marriage couldn't have been any better. We were perfect for each other. But now just a few issues can really stir up trouble and then we don't seem to be able to get ourselves out of it.

I'd love to have it back they way we were at the beginning.

Anne Marie's score = 8
Matthew's score = 7

Our Analysis

Notice the difference in tone of each of these couples. Can you see a difference?

Gary and Susan have bitterness and indifference as part of the scenario. Neither said that their beginning was wonderful. In fact, Gary described an imbalance in their desire for the relationship for a considerable time at the beginning. We wonder just how much bitterness is left because he brushed off Susan in the beginning of their relationship. Gary sounds like he got used to Susan and when they were apart he missed the convenience of the relationship so he decided they should get married.
They are having infrequent sex at this time and even when they have it – it isn't fun and pleasure –

it's just getting it over with.

When you're describing the way you match on these differences that make a difference, you must consider how you match now, how you matched at the beginning, and consider whether any change in match is related to temporary circumstances or to permanent, more far-reaching differences.

Unfortunately, sexual expression and demonstrations of affection don't seem to have added much to this couple's marriage and the added stress in their marriage is making it worse. The differences in their sexual needs are part of the problem.

Susan needs to discern if her lack of sexual desire is because of her dislike for and bitterness toward Gary, whether she just naturally has less of a sex drive overall, because she's exhausted from the stress and work of daily life, and/or because she's already getting enough attention and physical touching from her children that she doesn't want anymore from her husband.

Whereas, Anne Marie and Matthew both express how wonderful their sexual lives have been with each other. Even though they're having less sex at this time, it's still good for them. There's a sense that good sex and demonstrations of affection are adding strength to their struggling marriage rather than further taxing it.

Describe Yourself

Age – What is your age?

_____

_____

_____

_____

Describe Your Partner

Age – What is his or her age?

_____

_____

_____

_____

Score the Match from 1 (no match)
to 10 (best match)

Examples

Couple #1
Gary's answer: I'm 38. The only thing our age difference may do is that I think Susan isn't quite as mature in some ways.

Susan's answer: I am 34. Gary treats me like a child sometimes.

Gary's score = 9
Susan's score = 8

Couple #2
Anne Marie's answer: I'm 36. I don't think there is any age difference at all.

Matthew's answer: I'm 40 and we seem the same age to me. The only thing is that Anne Marie doesn't ever seem to worry about saving for retirement.

Anne Marie's score = 8
Matthew's score = 9

Our Analysis

The age range for both of these couples doesn't add to their problems. They are close enough in age to be able to relate to each other and to enjoy similar interests common to their era.

We can detect a problem for each, however. Susan feels like Gary treats her like a child. We'll have to see if this problem shows up anywhere else. We'll have to see whether Gary does or doesn't treat Susan like a child.

Matthew is expressing a wish that Anne Marie would take saving for retirement more seriously. We'll be on the lookout for more trouble in the area of spending and saving money for this couple.

Health and fitness, including the habits of smoking, drinking, or using drugs – What do you believe and practice in regard to taking care of yourself – your health and fitness? What is your diet? What is your exercise routine? Do you smoke? Do you drink alcohol? Do you use drugs? What do you think about those issues? How do you think health and fitness issues affect children?

_____

_____

_____

_____

_____

_____

_____

_____

_____

_____

_____

_____

_____

_____

_____

_____

_____

Describe Your Partner

_____

_____

_____

_____

_____

_____

_____

_____

_____

_____

_____

_____

_____

_____

_____

_____

_____

_____

_____

_____

**Score the Match from 1 (no match)
to 10 (best match)**

Examples

Couple #1

Gary's answer: I like to be physically active and because of that I don't have trouble with my health and weight. I wish Susan would exercise. She's getting pretty heavy and it isn't good for her and she doesn't look as attractive. In other ways, I think we match pretty well. We don't smoke at all and we don't drink much. We've never used drugs.

Susan's answer: Gary's always trying to get me to be more active. It really makes me mad because I'm tired after working all day and all week. I like to refresh myself by reading. He's off doing his physical activities and I'm stuck here doing laundry and cleaning the house trying to get organized for the next workweek. I'm careful about what I eat.

Gary's score = 9
Susan's score = 6

Couple #2

Anne Marie's answer: I don't think we have much of a difference here, but I do like to be more active. I worry about Matthew's health a little bit. He needs to lose a little weight. Otherwise we match very well.

Matthew's answer: We match very well on this difference. I should lose a little weight. And I would like more physical activity if I weren't so busy at work all of the time. After all of the traveling and stress I just feel like being at home. I know Anne Marie would like to do more, but I won't feel much like it until my work schedule settles down some.

Anne Marie's score = 7
Matthew's score = 8

Our Analysis

We detect some parenting in Gary's tone and wonder if it doesn't add to Susan's feelings that she gets treated like a child. Even if Gary is right about her getting more exercise, he sounds like a bit of a scold. This alone isn't much, but added to other things may be part of a pattern. Does Gary see himself as having all of the answers?

Also, note the discrepancy between Gary's and Susan's scoring. Gary sees them closer together on their match than Susan sees them. Is that wishful thinking on Gary's part or is it that he doesn't see his criticism of Susan's weight that big a deal? Either way this is adding to a stressful climate. If Gary has trouble seeing the reality of their relationship and keeps trying to make it seem better than it is, he's just living dishonestly. If his attitude is part of an overall sense of his knowing more and better than Susan and a parenting tone with her, you can imagine how Susan must resent being parented rather than being an equal partner.

Gary's concern about his wife's weight isn't bad in itself. Susan's health is important. But as part of a troubled marriage and within the context of a bad relationship it's adding another layer of trouble.

The point is neither Gary nor Susan are wrong about what to do to rest and refresh themselves – they're just different. Health is a reflection of how people regard themselves and therefore, how they take care of themselves. The fact is that some people are much more relaxed about these issues than others. Gary interprets Susan's behavior as disregarding him, herself, and her health. Susan regards her actions as in her best interest.

Anne Marie and Matthew have a slight difference, but nothing that inspires the other to feel challenged about themselves. They also score themselves within a point of each other. No problem with this difference.

Describe Yourself

Where to live – Where do you want to live? Do you have allergies or other health reasons for living in certain areas? How flexible are you about where you want to live? Will your career influence where you live? What climates are most conducive to your well being? Do you enjoy leisure activities that require proximity to certain climates or terrain? Does it matter how close you live to your extended family?

_____

_____

_____

_____

_____

_____

_____

_____

_____

_____

_____

_____

_____

_____

_____

_____

_____

Describe Your Partner

_____

_____

_____

_____

_____

_____

_____

_____

_____

_____

_____

_____

_____

_____

_____

_____

_____

_____

_____

_____

**Score the Match from 1 (no match)
to 10 (best match)**

Examples

Couple #1
Gary's answer: We basically agree on where we want to live.

Susan's answer: We are way over our head financially to be living in the house we live in. It's like we live our entire lives to live in our house.

Earlier in our marriage I moved here to be with Gary far from my family and friends. I felt stranded and alone until I got a job. Now I feel better about living here, but I didn't in the beginning.

Gary's score = 8
Susan's score = 6

Couple #2
Anne Marie's answer: We agree exactly on where we want to live.

Matthew's answer: We both want to live right where we live.

Anne Marie's score = 10
Matthew's score = 10

Our Analysis

Gary and Susan have another problem here. Susan sounds resentful about living above their means. She also harbors some sentiment about having moved away from her family and friends even though she says she's okay about it now.

Alone this doesn't sound like too much of a problem. Probably manageable. But in the context of
the other problems, Susan construes living above
their means as her not knowing enough to be satisfied. She doesn't think Gary holds her opinion in
high enough regard. Gary would rather spend his
money this way and Susan would rather have more
money for other goods. She feels trapped by the big
mortgage.

Anne Marie and Matthew have added support from
their agreement on where to live.

Describe Yourself

Education/Intelligence – To what level of education do you aspire? What are your beliefs about education and intelligence? What are your intellectual interests? What do you like to talk about? What topics spark your curiosity?

_____

_____

_____

_____

_____

_____

_____

_____

_____

_____

_____

_____

_____

_____

_____

_____

_____

_____

Describe Your Partner

_____

_____

_____

_____

_____

_____

_____

_____

_____

_____

_____

_____

_____

_____

_____

_____

_____

_____

**Score the Match from 1 (no match)
to 10 (best match)**

Examples

Couple #1
Gary's answer: I went further in school than Susan did. Maybe that's part of the reason that Susan just doesn't understand how to handle and spend money right and what's important. But I think Susan is happy with what I do and the lifestyle it provides.

I like to talk about my work and the children.

Susan's answer: Gary has a professional degree and I have a college degree. I think we're matched intellectually, but I think Gary believes that he's smarter than I am. But the thing about this difference that really bothers me is that Gary doesn't like to read at all. It's like when he finished school he thought that learning was finished. I'm constantly reading and working on self-improvement and he doesn't want to talk about what I read and it's like he thinks he's a finished product. He resents my reading and believes I should attend to him instead.

Gary's score = 9
Susan's score = 9

Couple #2
Anne Marie's answer: We're very well matched in this area. I can't think of any difference.

Matthew's answer: I can't see any difference at all between us. I think Ann Marie is just as smart as I am, but I wish she'd take saving some money more seriously. She thinks money will just fall out of the sky. I make a huge income and she spends it all.

She makes a good income from her own business, but she spends it all. She just doesn't get it. We have to save some money.

Our Analysis

Did you hear it again? Gary and Susan have some serious issues going on here.

Once more we hear a sense of Gary relating to Susan as the child and he the parent. It's beginning to show itself as a pattern. They have differences that make a difference and they don't have good relationship skills, which compounds their problems.

They have another difference in continuing education, so to speak. They are matched intellectually, but have different interests so they don't have much to talk about. Susan isn't interested in what Gary talks about so she turns him off. Gary thinks Susan just doesn't know as much as he does and he treats their differences as though he's right and she's wrong. That adds another layer upon the other layers. Blaming the other only builds resentment. Being different is just that – being different. Being different isn't right or wrong, it's just being different.

Anne Marie and Matthew seem to have a different problem. Again, they're well matched, but they do seem to have a problem agreeing on how to spend their money. We'll have to see what they have to say when we look at how they believe and practice money management. Their ability to respect each other's intelligence adds strength to their marriage.

Lifestyle (Formal versus Informal, active versus passive) – Do you like to take off your shoes and put your feet up? Do you like everything in its place or is your home a place to let your hair down? Would you rather entertain at a backyard barbecue or a dinner party? Are you child and family oriented or career and philanthropically oriented? Do you enjoy activities requiring passivity or would you rather be physically active? How do you balance formal and informal aspects of your life? How do you balance activity and passivity?

_____

_____

_____

_____

_____

_____

_____

_____

_____

_____

_____

_____

_____

_____

_____

Describe Your Partner

_____

_____

_____

_____

_____

_____

_____

_____

_____

_____

_____

_____

_____

_____

_____

_____

_____

_____

**Score the Match from 1 (no match)
to 10 (best match)**

Examples

Couple #1

Gary's answer: I'm basically a casual, active person. Susan and I match very well in that we both enjoy a casual life rather than a more formal lifestyle. We both enjoy watching our children play sports and go to their games regularly. We enjoy friendships with our neighbors and parents of the children that ours play with.

Susan's answer: Gary and I both like casual living. He's more active and I'm more passive. We're definitely child and family oriented.

Gary's score = 8
Susan's score = 9

Couple #2

Anne Marie's answer: We both like to live casually. In the beginning we both liked activity, but lately Matthew hasn't wanted to do much of anything. I can't get him to take us anywhere or do anything. He wants to be with the kids and me but only at home. I work at home and I'm dying to get out sometimes. We're children oriented, but sometimes Matthew has to attend formal business functions, which he doesn't like very much.

Matthew's answer: We like to live casually. Unfortunately, Anne Marie would love to do more when I'm not working, but I'm so tired I can't stand to leave the house. I just like to sit home with my family. If I didn't work so hard and travel so much, I'd want to go out more. I have to go to some formal events, but I don't like them very much. I like spending time with my family. I feel bad about disappointing my wife and I would like to go more places, but I just can't right now.

Anne Marie's score = 10
Matthew's score = 6

Our Analysis

Gary and Susan's match on this difference helps them stay together. They do enjoy similar lifestyles, which adds some level of comfort to their lives. Their desire for similar lifestyles is one of the things that attracted them to each other. Their desire for the lifestyle they live keeps them together and returning to each other after a major rift.

Anne Marie and Matthew also match well. Matthew has scored their match much less than it really is because they have a temporary difference in drive for going to outside activities. He shows evidence of regretting that he can't spend as much time having fun with his wife and children. He's having some difficulty balancing his work and recreational activity. Ann Marie has a tendency to interpret his wanting to stay home in a personal way and believes he's lost interest in having fun with her.

Anne Marie and Matthew view this as a temporary situation because they weren't this way before and they agree that they should work hard now and retire as early as possible. They both envision being together and enjoying each other in retirement. They may be emphasizing work more than they can survive. We'd recommend more balance. It won't do any good to retire early if they've ruined their relationship by growing distant or damaged their health.

Describe Yourself

Views about work/Level of ambition – What are your career ambitions? What work do you do or what work would you like to do? What hours do you work? What would be the ideal balance of work and play to you? What kind of an income will it take to support the lifestyle you desire?

_____

_____

_____

_____

_____

_____

_____

_____

_____

_____

_____

_____

_____

_____

_____

_____

_____

Describe Your Partner

_____

_____

_____

_____

_____

_____

_____

_____

_____

_____

_____

_____

_____

_____

_____

_____

_____

_____

**Score the Match from 1 (no match)
to 10 (best match)**

Examples

Couple #1
Gary's answer: One of the things that upset me the most over the past few years, and actually that started all of this to some degree, is that Susan changed her job. She had this great job and we had major financial commitments and she quit the job to take a job with a serious pay cut. Not only that, but I'd been able to be with the children more. Now I have to work harder and longer and she has it much easier. She really messed things up when she changed her job.

Susan's answer: I like the lifestyle that our work supports and I think we're very well matched in terms of work balanced with the rest of our lives.

A couple of years ago I had to change my job, but I decreased my stress level so much by doing it, even with a pay cut, it was well worth the change. The change has been a bone of contention between Gary and me, but I had to do it. Before I had to get up before dawn, get ready for work, get the kids set for school, and drive 35 minutes or more to get to work. I just couldn't take the stress of the commute on top of the work of my job and my family. I'm much better off now, but you'd think I murdered someone the way Gary carries on about it. All he thinks about is himself. He didn't have to work as hard before, but I never got to see my kids. And I was exhausted all of the time. I'm still tired, but not to the degree that I was. Does he think he's the only one to consider? I need to be with the kids sometimes, too.

Gary's score = 5
Susan's score = 10

Couple #2

Anne Marie's answer: I think we're pretty well matched here. I wish Matthew didn't have to work and travel so much. But it's temporary and we should be able to retire earlier than usual. Lately, his travel has given me rest from our arguments.

Matthew's answer: We have similar ambition and drive to succeed at work and in our personal lives. We have similar goals and want the same lifestyle. I don't think Anne Marie appreciates the amount of money we make in the same way I do and she scares me the way she spends every cent that we make.

Anne Marie has a wonderful sales ability. Everyone loves her. She has a great business of her own going, but she doesn't realize how good it is and how good it could be if she'd run it like a business rather than having it for fun. Every time I suggest she add some structure she has a fit because she thinks I want to just take it over.

Anne Marie's score = 7
Matthew's score = 8

Our Analysis

Gary and Susan's answers to this question begin to show the degree of animosity between them. Actually, Susan doesn't spend as much time dwelling and noticing all of the details, so she doesn't recognize the differences here between her husband and her. That in itself is a misrepresentation of reality.

Gary has a more realistic perception of the difference, but his problem is that he sees his way as the right way. His goal is to change his wife into doing things his way, which is what makes Susan feel so bad all of the time. It's what makes her so angry with Gary. Why should she have to give herself up to be married?

Gary's anger that he had to work longer hours when Susan changed her job is further indication of a problem. Is Gary self-centered and wanting others to take care of him so he won't have to work as hard? Does his welfare come before his wife's? Does he compete with his wife for his children's affection? Why does he resent his wife's desire to mother her children? All are subtle clues about definite problems in this marriage.

When we explored some of the issues that surfaced here, we also got a glimpse of a serious money difference between them. We learned that Gary handles his money separate from his wife and Susan doesn't even know how much he makes. We'll explore that further when we discuss managing money.

Anne Marie and Matthew have a minor problem here, but it's temporary. The issues that surfaced around Anne Marie's managing her business are related to unfinished business from her past and can be resolved. These two have strengths in their relationship that allows this difference to be diminished. Since Anne Marie's resistance to her husband's input about her business is related to her past, there's a strong possibility that she can come to terms with it and let her husband offer his excellent business advice more often without feeling as though he'll just take over.

Matthew has an assertive and a rather bold manner, which hides his sensitive nature. He's also passionate about his ideas. It reminds Anne Marie of her troubled past at times and she shuts down whenever he comes on boldly. As he recognizes that his manner triggers an age regression for Anne Marie, he can contribute a change in the dynamic by changing his response – something that's easy for him to do because he feels love, tenderness, and respect for his wife.

Anne Marie will feel less threatened by Matthew's assertive and passionate manner when she can disengage her automatic reaction and remind herself that Matthew isn't the person that hurt her so much as a child. When she feels less threatened, her behavior will change and their interaction around these issues will calm.

An asset in the marriage is Anne Marie and Matthew's equal gift for business. She wants to perform well and she wants recognition for a job well done. Part of her defense to the hurt in her past has been to become competitive. Anne Marie excels at competition. All of this is to her advantage in the business world, but it's a problem in her marriage. Competition between marriage partners doesn't work. But this problem is related to her past and can be moderated with a little work.

An improvement in relationship skills and healing of old emotional wounds will resolve this difference. They really aren't very different at all.

Describe Yourself

Views on how to handle and spend money – How do you want to spend, save, and invest? What are your short- and long-term financial goals? What meanings do you attach to money? Who pays the bills? Who controls the money?

_____

_____

_____

_____

_____

_____

_____

_____

_____

_____

_____

_____

_____

_____

_____

_____

_____

Describe Your Partner

_____

_____

_____

_____

_____

_____

_____

_____

_____

_____

_____

_____

_____

_____

_____

_____

_____

_____

**Score the Match from 1 (no match)
to 10 (best match)**

Examples

Couple #1

Gary's answer: Susan just doesn't have an appreciation of money. She just spends and spends. Before we were married I tried to combine finances and immediately had three bounced checks. I decided then and there that I couldn't live that way and separated my money from Susan's. She shows me the bills and I give her some money each month to help her pay her bills. I can't get her to stop spending money.

Susan's answer: Gary doesn't understand how much it costs to clothe the children and run the house. He's completely unrealistic about the household budget. He doesn't tell me how much he makes. He treats me like a child. When I bounced those checks, I had never managed a checkbook before. I was young and inexperienced. Instead of helping me learn how to manage the money he just took it away and used the issue as another way to control me. I can't describe how much anger and rage I feel toward him about how he treats me like a child. I can hardly stand to look at him at times.

I hate being financially strapped. I wish we'd sell the house so we didn't have all of our money tied up in it. Gary says we don't have enough money, but every time I turn around he has money to spend on something he wants – like furniture. He just doesn't have money for the things I want. He sees one piece of furniture that we were looking for and he buys several pieces impulsively rather than the one piece that we wanted. Something doesn't fit here. Just because he says it's my entire fault doesn't mean that it is. I think he's a control freak and he doesn't want to share. I'm tired of it.

Another thing is that he exaggerates so much I can never tell when what he says is true or not. He exaggerates so much I'm embarrassed. He exaggerates to me and in social situations.

Gary's score = 5
Susan's score = 6

Couple #2

Anne Marie's answer: I want to retire early and spend the rest of my life with Matthew. We'll have plenty of money. He'll get a bonus at a certain time, which will be plenty. Besides, he makes me so mad. He spends plenty of money on his daughter. Spending money is one way I can pay him back for how mad he makes me.

Matthew's answer: We make plenty of money, but we spend every cent of it. I just want Anne Marie to help me save some so we can retire early and run our own businesses and travel – have some fun together. I love the way she decorates the house. But she gives the children too much. They get anything they want and then some. They have so much stuff they lose interest in what they have.

Look, I think my daughter (this college age daughter is from a previous marriage) should have my help until she gets out of college. I realize giving her a free ride doesn't help her become independent, but when you're in college you have to depend on some help. I did pay off her credit cards this once, but only this once. I won't do it again. Anne Marie is so jealous of her.

Our Analysis

The depth of Susan's resentment really shows itself here. And managing the money in this marriage illuminates Gary's need for control and dominance. Gary complains that his wife won't have sex with him, but how can a daughter have sex with her father? "Gasp," you say. But Gary is more interested in fathering Susan than in being her partner and mate.

Lack of mature emotional development and poor relationship skills are creating havoc in this marriage, but underlying that is a difference that really makes a difference. Susan doesn't want to tie up all of their money to live so extravagantly. She doesn't see the point in depriving themselves day to day to live beyond their means. If living in their house means deprivation and stress, she'd rather not live there. Gary, on the other hand, is concerned about appearances and assets. And again, he blames Susan for having mixed up values. A double whammy. They have a difference, but from Gary's perspective, her way is the bad way.

With Anne Marie and Matthew, we can see a monstrous issue raised to the surface that gets played out with money. Anne Marie is jealous of Matthew's daughter from his previous marriage.

In exploring the issue of Anne Marie's jealousy, we discovered that there is a small basis for the jealousy in that Matthew has some guilt about leaving his daughter and is somewhat over-invested in her life – not much, but a little. And we also uncovered a seriously destructive competition in Anne Marie's childhood home between her sister and herself – that her mother fueled. And more competition with her mother over getting so much of her father and paternal grandmother's attention. The destructive interactions had left their mark on Anne Marie and whenever something happened that had a competitive element, Anne Marie age regressed with all of the attending emotional baggage. The age regression left Anne Marie unable to handle the current circumstance in the here and now and with competence. Knowing the reason for the intensity of her response – naming what happened – changed the dynamic forever and with some practice Anne Marie was able to grow into handling the situation in a more productive manner. Everyone benefited.

Gary could also work through the issues that have left him so controlling and paternalistic, but he must let down his defenses and recognize what he does first. Even if he does the work necessary to heal himself and liberates himself to relate in a more adult way to Susan, they still have differences in how they want to manage their money.

Anne Marie and Matthew have already repaired their money problem. Money was being used to handle the jealousy as a payback and there is no longer a need for that so money suddenly doesn't present itself as a problem.

Describe Yourself

Expectations of marriage – How much time do you want to spend with your partner? Do you want to be best friends or share confidences with other best friends, too? What do you believe about male and female roles in a marriage and a family? What do you expect marriage to provide for you?

_____

_____

_____

_____

_____

_____

_____

_____

_____

_____

_____

_____

_____

_____

_____

Describe Your Partner

_____

_____

_____

_____

_____

_____

_____

_____

_____

_____

_____

_____

_____

_____

_____

_____

_____

_____

_____

**Score the Match from 1 (no match)
to 10 (best match)**

Examples

Couple #1

Gary's answer: I want my wife to be my companion and friend. Susan wants the same thing. The only thing that ever gets in the way with this issue is that when Susan is tired she wants to read. I can't watch TV because it bothers her. And she won't interact with me so I feel lonely. I have to spend my free time at home in another room.

Susan's answer: I think we're pretty well matched here. We both want to be a companion to each other and we want to be friends. We have a difficult time doing it because we fight so much. How can I be a best friend with my husband when he sees me as less than him? We want the same thing, but it's impossible to have.

Gary's score = 8
Susan's score = 10

Couple #2

Anne Marie's answer: We both want to be with each other the same. We are each other's best friends. Lately, though, I'm relieved when Matthew travels because I get to do things my way and there isn't any fighting. I miss him, but when he's back home life gets difficult again.

Matthew's answer: I want Anne Marie to be my best friend and spend my leisure time with her and my kids. We have fun together and I like doing things with her. I would like Anne Marie to see to dinner and manage the household a little more tightly. She doesn't take her business very seriously so I don't think it's too much to ask for her to have dinner for us when I get home.

Our Analysis

Unless Gary can resolve the issues that compel him to treat Susan like a child, he'll never get to have the best friend and companion in Susan that he says he wants. This could be a source of strength in their marriage, but Gary's way of relating makes it impossible. It's interesting to note that Susan has some very clear differences with Gary, but she scores them high consistently. Just for your information – sometime into their therapy, Susan suddenly stated that she'd not taken the 16 differences seriously enough. That they really make a huge difference and she had just quickly brushed them off. She was beginning to see that you couldn't deceive yourself about them. Even if you score yourselves high, if it isn't true, it continues to be a problem. You can't wish your problems away.

Matthew is also accustomed to giving direction and orders at work. He carries his role over into his family life just a little too much. He wouldn't meet with resistance to Anne Marie's doing the household management like having dinner ready, if he would trust her and let her run the show. She's extremely competent and without the fighting over some of the issues they've encountered, Anne Marie would take pride in running the house. Because Anne Marie and Matthew are basically compatible, they'll be able to work this out with some minor adjustments. When the jealousy issue got resolved, most of this kind of arguing stopped.

Describe Yourself

Physical characteristics attractive to you – What about looks are important to you? What does your perfect partner look like? Are there certain body types or features that turn you on more than others? What styles of clothing do you admire?

_____

_____

_____

_____

_____

_____

_____

_____

_____

_____

_____

_____

_____

_____

_____

_____

_____

_____

Describe Your Partner

_____

_____

_____

_____

_____

_____

_____

_____

_____

_____

_____

_____

_____

_____

_____

_____

_____

_____

**Score the Match from 1 (no match)
to 10 (best match)**

Examples

Couple #1
Gary's answer: I'm very attracted to Susan and I think she is to me. I do wish she'd exercise and lose some weight.

Susan's answer: I used to be attracted to Gary. Now he repulses me. I'm so angry with him for years of treating me like a child that I don't even want to look at him.

Gary's score = 8
Susan's score = 8

Couple #2
Anne Marie's answer: I'm very attracted to my husband when I'm not mad at him. Sometimes I can't even look at him I'm so mad.

Matthew's answer: I'm very attracted to Anne Marie, but I don't think she's attracted to me.

Our Analysis

Attraction cannot go on forever when resentment and bad feelings build. Even when you have good compatibility, if you do something that erodes trust and warm and friendly feelings, over time, you'll lose any chance of recapturing the love. You must protect the friendly and warm feelings with your life.

Attraction is very important, but it isn't everything.

Religious beliefs and practices – Religion itself is not the issue here. Your beliefs and practices are the issue. What are your religious beliefs and practices? How do you want to raise any children in regard to religious beliefs and practices? What part does spirituality play in your life?

_____

_____

_____

_____

_____

_____

_____

_____

_____

_____

_____

_____

_____

_____

_____

_____

_____

Describe Your Partner

_____

_____

_____

_____

_____

_____

_____

_____

_____

_____

_____

_____

_____

_____

_____

_____

_____

_____

**Score the Match from 1 (no match)
to 10 (best match)**

Examples

Couple #1
Gary's answer: Neither of us is religious. We agree on not having religion play a part in our lives to any large degree.

Susan's answer: We're not religious and we agree on the part religion does not play in our lives.

Gary's score = 8
Susan's score = 10

Couple #2
Anne Marie's answer: I think religion should play a larger role in our lives. We're both Catholic and I would like us to have some family religious time together.

Matthew's answer: I think we agree on raising the children in the Catholic Church and on the fact that neither of us likes going to church much.

Our Analysis

As long as they are both being honest about what they believe and want in regard to religion, Gary and Susan are okay here.

Anne Marie and Matthew discovered some contention with this issue and had an opportunity to revisit the issue. They didn't have any trouble working out what they wanted.

A word about religion and spiritual beliefs. Many people have had religious dogma stuffed down their throats by hypocrites that don't practice what they say in their own lives. As a result, they've turned away from their traditional roots. And as science has shown a practical and objective means of collecting information about the world, it has reinforced a "who needs religion" position.

Unfortunately, by throwing the baby out with the bath water, many people have given up a major support system for individuals and families. We would recommend a reexamination of beliefs by thinking for yourself and making sure that you live your values. Going to church isn't what's at issue – although spiritual communities have value – but having a framework of values from which to live and practicing what your values dictate is the issue. Everyone benefits personally from values and maintaining their integrity by living their values. And all of our families and communities benefit from individuals that live with integrity.

Political beliefs and practices – What are your
political beliefs and practices? What part does politics play in your life?

_____

_____

_____

_____

_____

_____

_____

_____

_____

_____

_____

_____

_____

_____

_____

_____

_____

_____

_____

_____

Describe Your Partner

_____

_____

_____

_____

_____

_____

_____

_____

_____

_____

_____

_____

_____

_____

_____

_____

_____

_____

**Score the Match from 1 (no match)
to 10 (best match)**

Examples

Couple #1

Gary's answer: We never talk about politics. I'm probably a bit more conservative than Susan is, but politics isn't very important to either of us so we don't have any open disagreements about it. Sometimes I wonder if Susan's feminist beliefs are a further indication that she just doesn't like men much. Her family is full of women that don't like men.

Susan's answer: Politics don't matter to me or to Gary. Politics isn't an issue with us. It's interesting that Gary says my family is full of women that don't like men. His sister is gay and his mother spends all of her free time hanging out with his sister and her friends. He describes his smooth upbringing by saying there wasn't any conflict. He says they talked things over and found non-conflictual ways of "getting around my mother" who was constantly combative and hostile.

Gary's score = 7
Susan's score = 9

Couple #2

Anne Marie's answer: Neither of us is interested in politics.

Matthew's answer: We don't talk about politics because we don't care much one way or the other.

Anne Marie's score = 8
Matthew's score = 10

Our Analysis

Again, if our couples are being honest and accurate, they're in reasonable shape here, although, Gary and Susan have another pool of hostility. The issue of sexual identity seems to be an issue. Neither seems to have any confusion about their own sexual identity, but their role models have undoubtedly influenced their family dynamics, which, in turn, influenced them individually.

The important thing to consider is that, once again, Gary has announced that Susan is wrong. It is a serious problem that they can't just own differences, but that there is a right and wrong way to think or feel. In a relationship like this, there isn't room for the other person. That's the relationship skill part of their conflict. The differences they have are incompatibility problems.

Just a quick word about politics. Political beliefs and practices represent your view about the world. At least, if you've thought for yourself and don't just vote the way your parents voted. Don't kid yourself that politics doesn't affect your life. If you examine political ideology – just America's two parties – it represents a profoundly different way of relating to the world and other people. An individual's psychology and politics fit very closely together if you've really examined the ideas for yourself. Not being interested in politics says something about someone's level of maturity and their taking or not taking responsibility for their lives. It pays to have personal power in your life and exerting the personal power you have through political practices is part of freedom and liberty. Exercising that freedom and liberty takes willingness to take responsibility.

Describe Yourself

Children – Having them and raising them – Do you want children? How many and when? Describe your disciplinary style. Describe parental roles. What does parenting mean to you?

_____

_____

_____

_____

_____

_____

_____

_____

_____

_____

_____

_____

_____

_____

_____

_____

_____

_____

_____

Describe Your Partner

_____

_____

_____

_____

_____

_____

_____

_____

_____

_____

_____

_____

_____

_____

_____

_____

_____

_____

**Score the Match from 1 (no match)
to 10 (best match)**

Examples

Couple #1

Gary's answer: We wanted to have three children and that's what we've had. One thing that Susan does that really upsets me is that she diminishes my credibility in front of the children by making fun of things I say to them or some remark designed to make me look bad.

Susan's answer: We agreed to have three children and we did. I think we basically agree on how to raise the children and what values we want them to have. I do come off critical about Gary in front of the children, but so does he about me. He hammers on me and criticizes me in front of them all of the time. He exaggerates so much that I have to help the children with a reality check. I'm so angry at him most of the time that sometimes I really show my hostility. I know it isn't good for the kids, but I can't seem to help myself.

Gary's score = 9
Susan's score = 10

Couple #2

Anne Marie's answer: We have the number of kids we want, but I don't like the way Matthew yells at the children. He scares them. I don't want them to feel the way I did growing up – always being afraid and hurt. He'd never touch them, but when he yells it scares us all.

Matthew's answer: We both wanted two children. We really do get into some fights about the children. I think Anne Marie is too easy on them and gives them too much. When I try to get them to do what I want she gets in the middle. She thinks I favor my older daughter over our kids, but it just isn't true. I think kids need discipline and limits. How are they going to function in the world unless we teach them what they need to know? If they can get everything without working for it, how will they ever learn to value what they have? How will they learn to work for what they want? We definitely need some help in this area. Besides money, this is the issue that we have the most trouble with.

Anne Marie's score = 5
Matthew's score = 5

Our Analysis

Notice that both couples agree with each other about their scores. Also notice that for the degree of difficulty that each couple describes that Anne Marie and Matthew are scoring themselves the most realistically. Gary and Susan describe a serious problem in raising their children – namely, that Susan's anger at Gary inspires her to undermine his authority with them. This behavior will have a devastating affect on the children. And yet, they've scored themselves "9". Unrealistic. Anne Marie and Matthew recognize and accurately score a serious problem they're having raising their children. You can't fix something unless you can realistically appraise the problem. Emotionally developed, mature adults can realistically evaluate problems and solve them in a collaborative way. Gary and Susan's unrealistic scoring and wishful thinking is only postponing the inevitable recognition that they have a serious problem and that their marriage is on the line.

Raising children can bring your beliefs, practices,

and values to the forefront quickly. Learning to know a prospective partner about how they'll raise children is difficult when they haven't experienced being a parent. You can think you'll behave one way and then behave completely differently. But it's vital to attempt to get some idea of how a prospective partner will interact with children. As you may have learned in your marriage, when your styles of raising children are different it can be fertile ground for war.

Both these couple have serious issues in regard to raising their children. Both couple seem to want the same result from their upbringing. Both couples are allowing their anger to influence their styles of interaction with their children. Both families are suffering. Gary and Susan have so many differences mixed together with so much wishful thinking and inappropriate coping that their prognosis of saving the children from destructive conflict is remote. If they stay together the chances are high that one more generation will carry on with poor selection of marriage partners and poor marriages – at the very least. If they divorce and find better partners, remarry, and construct happier lives, their children will benefit by their parents breaking the cycle of destructive relationships. Sometimes staying in a bad marriage is far more destructive to the development of the children than leaving.

Anne Marie and Matthew have much more positive strength in their marriage. They have more with which to work. There is a very specific issue driving their differences in how to raise the children and that issue is amenable to correction. They are less defensive and have a more accurate picture of what's really happening, so they have what it takes to solve the problem constructively. The children in the family will benefit from their working out their problems and staying together.

Life stage – What is the focus of your life right now? Are you finishing school? Are you just beginning a career? Have you settled into your career? Are you raising children? Are you childless? Are you planning a career change? Are you planning for retirement?

_____

_____

_____

_____

_____

_____

_____

_____

_____

_____

_____

_____

_____

_____

_____

_____

_____

Describe Your Partner

_____

_____

_____

_____

_____

_____

_____

_____

_____

_____

_____

_____

_____

_____

_____

_____

_____

_____

_____

**Score the Match from 1 (no match)
to 10 (best match)**

Examples

Couple #1

Gary's answer: We're in identical life stages. We're both well into our careers and raising school age children.

Susan's answer: We're in the same life stage.

Gary's score = 8
Susan's score = 9

Couple #2

Anne Marie's answer: We're a tiny bit off on this difference, but I don't thing if makes much of a difference. Maybe a small difference. Matthew has an a college age daughter from a previous marriage. We're not that different in age, but I've never raised a child that age before so I'm sure I don't understand what it's like. And Matthew didn't live with his daughter during her school age years so he doesn't have any experience raising younger children. Matthew is into figuring out our retirement and I don't feel it's important right now. From what he's told me, I don't think we'll have a problem. Anyway, we do have a slight difference here. Talking about it may help both of us with the issues. I've never even thought about it from this perspective.

Matthew's answer: We're a little off here, but not so much that I think it will hurt us over the long run. Anne Marie doesn't understand what's important for a college age child, I don't think. And I think she's very good with our two children. In fact, she's with them so much more than I am, I really feel she knows what's best – most of the time. But she does give them too much. She also doesn't take planning for retirement seriously enough. I want to retire early and have a semi-retired second career. She's all for that, but she thinks the money for it will just sort of take care of itself. We need some help in this area, but I don't think it's a major problem.

Anne Marie's score = 10
Matthew's score = 8

Our Analysis

The synchronicity of Gary and Susan's life stage adds some stability to their marriage. It isn't enough, but it doesn't add another negative drain.

Anne Marie and Matthew have, once again, accurately recognized a minor difference in their life stages. It isn't as bad as it could be and won't have much impact on their marriage overall. They do need some assistance with better coping over the difference and a forum for working through the issues involved. We believe they'll be able to do that without much difficulty because they aren't very defensive, they're both highly motivated to stay married, and they have a very friendly and loving basis for doing so.

Common leisure interests – What do you do for fun? How do you balance fun and work? Do you like physical activity or would you rather read or watch TV or a movie? What balance of active and passive leisure activity do you like? What kind of activity recharges your batteries and refreshes you? Do you like solitary activity or would you rather spend your leisure with others? How many others? How much time do you devote to leisure? How much money do you devote to leisure? Do you like to plan your activities ahead of time or would you rather act spontaneously?

_____

_____

_____

_____

_____

_____

_____

_____

_____

_____

_____

_____

_____

_____

Describe Your Partner

_____

_____

_____

_____

_____

_____

_____

_____

_____

_____

_____

_____

_____

_____

_____

_____

_____

_____

**Score the Match from 1 (no match)
to 10 (best match)**

Examples

Couple #1

Gary's answer: We have a real problem here. Susan doesn't like to be physically active like I do. Her idea of a great day off is to lay around and read. I like to get outdoors and play sports. I've been trying to get Susan to get out and do stuff with me, but she's totally resistant to it.

Susan's answer: We don't like to do the same things when we're off from work. And to make matters worse, while Gary's off playing, I'm stuck home doing laundry and getting the family ready for the next workweek. He rarely helps – although he's done a little more recently. I don't know why he has to change me. Why can't he just leave me alone to do what I want?

Gary's score = 3
Susan's score = 9

Couple #2

Anne Marie's answer: We started out liking to do similar physical kinds of activities. But since Matthew started working so hard and travelling so much I can't get him to go out and do anything. I'd love to take the kids and go skiing and do other fun things, but all he wants to do is stay at home. I really do think he likes to do similar things that I like, but he's so tired of being away from home that he just wants to stay there. But what about me? What about having fun with me and the kids?

Matthew's answer: Ordinarily, I like to do the same things as my wife. Recently, I've traveled so much all I want to do is be at home with Anne

Marie and the children – one on each side of me watching TV or movies. I know Anne Marie wants to get out more, but I'm so tired of running around. I do think I should try harder to do more physically active things with the family. And I do try to get out alone with her as much as I can.

Anne Marie's score = 8
Matthew's score = 6

Our Analysis

Again, Gary and Susan add more negative drain to their relationship. As much time as we spend working, getting ready for work, and doing the business of the family, we don't have much time left for each other. And marriage bonds need nurturing. Most marriages cannot withstand just the work of life. Having fun together strengthens marital bonds. Gary and Susan do not add anything positive to the work of their life. Their marriage injects even more endless work just to get through the day. They've never had much common ground here.

Anne Marie and Matthew started out enjoying the same activities. They are in, what they hope, is a temporary stage where their ability to participate in the same activities is lessened. They both recognize the contributing factors. They haven't explored some things they could do to help themselves here that would lessen the strain. All of those factors demonstrate the possibility that this isn't going to harm their marriage and that they can find some temporary solutions until they can get back into a more relaxing and recreational time in their lives.

Energy levels – How much energy do you have? What time of the day do you have energy? What time of the day do you crash? Are you a night person or a day person? Do you have more or less mental or physical energy? How much energy do you have to be a companion and friend? How much energy do you have to be a parent?

_____

_____

_____

_____

_____

_____

_____

_____

_____

_____

_____

_____

_____

_____

_____

_____

_____

Describe Your Partner

_____

_____

_____

_____

_____

_____

_____

_____

_____

_____

_____

_____

_____

_____

_____

_____

_____

_____

**Score the Match from 1 (no match)
to 10 (best match)**

Examples

Couple #1

Gary's answer: Our energy levels are considerably different. I'm much more physically active and spend my energy being active. Susan is happiest reading. She doesn't have anywhere near the energy I have.

Susan's answer: Our energy levels match pretty closely. I spend my energy mentally rather than physically, so we're different that way, but not overall energy level.

Gary's score = 3
Susan's score = 8

Couple #2

Anne Marie's answer: We have similar energy levels.

Matthew's answer: I think Anne Marie has a little more energy than I have, but we're very close. In fact, we're probably about the same only I spend most of mine away from home where she spends most of hers at home with the kids and in her business.

Anne Marie's score = 8
Matthew's score = 7

Our Analysis

Not only do Gary and Susan have a difference in the way they spend their energy, but also, Gary sees Susan as having far less energy than he has.

Susan is correct to see that they have similar energy levels, but like to spend their energy differently. Gary believes that the right way is his way.

Anne Marie and Matthew aren't enjoying themselves as much as they did in the beginning of their relationship. If they can withstand the temporary stress of their work and life stage (raising kids takes most of your time and energy and that will lessen later) they'll probably bounce right back into their fun activities together. As long as they relieve some of the stress by going out together – alone – and doing some family activities they'll be okay. Again, they both recognize this and don't attack each other as being wrong, just in a different place. They'll have to take care not to grow apart.

You still have to evaluate life/relationship skills and attraction, but determining your level of compatibility on these 16 differences that make a difference is the crux of what you must know. Without compatibility on these issues that challenge integrity, it doesn't matter what your level of mastery is on the following relationship skills. Without compatibility on the differences all you can hope for is a marriage of convenience. Without a high level of compatibility on these 16 differences you'll spend most of your time and energy working on your marriage to limp along and your children will have to choose loyalties on important values and practices. Your children will learn to have the kind of marriage that you have.

Gary and Susan are in deep trouble in their marriage. They don't have much with which to work. They are very different in important ways and Gary, especially, believes his way is the best way. The marriage is particularly destructive to Susan. Gary would be much happier with someone that shared his view of how to live life. They could both enjoy the freedom to become themselves in an emotionally safe environment that adds to their lives rather than draining all of their time and energy if they were to divorce. We'd advise their separating and giving each other and their children an opportunity for happiness. We believe this is a case where the children would be far better off with their parents divorcing.

Anne Marie and Matthew have so much with which to work. They do have a few issues that must be worked out – or over time – they'll erode the good will and wonderful feelings they have for each other.

The cases of the two couples above are good examples of what you're trying to find out. What exactly do you have to work with?

The next thing to do is to add your total scores for matching on each of the 16 differences that make a difference.

Use the following score sheet.

1. How well do you match with your partner on the 16 differences that make a difference?

Don't match = 1   Match completely = 10
(Or any number in between one and ten that best describes your match)

Differences that Make a Difference	Score
Sex drives/sexual interests/demonstrations of affection	
Age	
Health & Fitness, including smoking, drinking, and/or using drugs	
Where to live	
Education/Intelligence	
Lifestyle	
Views about work/Level of ambition	
Views on how to handle and spend money	
Expectations of marriage/relationship	
Physical characteristics attractive to you	
Religion	
Politics	
Children: Having them and raising them	
Life stage	
Common leisure interests	
Energy levels	

Total = _____

If your score is:

Less than 80
Don't even consider this a good match

80-130
You are settling for less than the best

130-160
This is the range where you have the best chance to have a great marriage

Notes

_____

_____

_____

_____

_____

_____

_____

_____

_____

_____

_____

_____

_____

_____

Couple #1

Differences that Make a Difference	Gary's Score	Susan's Score
Sex drives/sexual interests/demonstrations of affection	2	5
Age	9	8
Health & Fitness, including smoking, drinking, and/or using drugs	9	6
Where to live	8	6
Education/Intelligence	9	9
Lifestyle	8	9
Views about work/Level of ambition	5	10
Views on how to handle and spend money	5	6
Expectations of marriage/Relationship	8	10
Physical characteristics attractive to you	8	8
Religion	8	10
Politics	7	9
Children: Having and raising them	9	10
Life stage	8	9
Common leisure interests	3	9
Energy levels	3	8
Total =	**109**	**132**

Our Comments

Compare the disparity in scores between Gary and Susan. Not only do they have critical differences, but also their perception of what's happening is completely different. It's interesting to note that Susan recognized later that she hadn't taken the 16 differences seriously enough – that they made a real difference. She also hadn't been very attentive to how many differences they really had – she'd discounted their differences. As she worked through issues in their marriage she realized her scoring had been inaccurate.

Gary's score is more accurate, but he's also the one that wants to keep trying. He believes that Susan hasn't really tried at all. If only she would really try, making the changes Gary thinks she should make, they'd be fine. Gary and Susan both have a lot of wishful thinking mixed up in their thinking.

Another thing to notice is that it only takes one or two serious mismatches to ruin the relationship. All 16 differences are important.

Gary and Susan may be able to grow in their emotional development and learn to handle their differences in a less destructive way, but they'll never change their underlying sex drives, their energy levels, or their leisure interests. At best, they can achieve a marriage of convenience – parallel play.

Couple #2

Differences that Make a Difference	Anne Marie's Score	Matthew's Score
Sex drives/sexual interests/ demonstrations of affection	8	7
Age	8	9
Health & Fitness, including smoking, drinking, and/ or using drugs	7	8
Where to live	10	10
Education/Intelligence	8	7
Lifestyle	10	6
Views about work/Level of ambition	7	8
Views on how to handle and spend money	6	1
Expectations of marriage/ Relationship	7	7
Physical characteristics attractive to you	7	8
Religion	5	10
Politics	8	10
Children: Having and raising them	5	5
Life stage	10	8
Common leisure interests	8	6
Energy levels	6	7
Total =	**120**	**117**

Our Comments

Anne Marie and Matthew agree overall. You can see exactly where their problems lie. We think that their differences wouldn't be such differences if some unfinished business were resolved for each partner. And their differences are related to temporary circumstances. Notice that their scores are only 15-20% better than Gary and Susan, which makes all of the difference in the world. They also have better coping skills so they haven't spiraled down into a hostile black hole of resentment. However, their scores are low enough that, without serious attention to what's wrong, in not too distant a future, they might also be divorcing.

Anne Marie and Matthew have much more going for their marriage. Their ability to resolve their past issues and get them out of their marriage will portend the success of their marriage.

Now What?

Let's look at the remaining four questions. The qualities of individuals that these questions represent contribute crucially to your marriage. Without the compatibility of matching on the 16 differences, these qualities can contribute positively toward peaceful coexistence and parallel play, or they can contribute destructively, dragging your marriage into a black hole of abusive interactions.

Marriage is for adults and the characteristics represented by these four questions are a result of mature emotional development.

Question 2: How effective is your partner?

By effective we mean effective as Stephen Covey defines effective in *The Seven Habits of Highly Effective People*, (Fireside/Simon & Schuster Inc., 1989).

Please see Covey's book for detailed explanations of the seven habits. While Covey writes of effectiveness in your work life, and he later wrote about effectiveness in families, being effective applies to all areas of your life. Effectiveness is an adult skill that you must have to operate at top function.

To understand how being effective applies specifically to the task of finding your perfect partner, see our book, *Perfect Partners™: Make Your Hopes and Dreams for a Great Marriage Come True.*

Effective people:
-Are able to define what is important
-Are able to accomplish worthwhile goals
-Lead rich, rewarding, and balanced lives

Ineffective people:
-Have too much to do in too little time
-Are busy doing mostly unimportant things
-May succeed in one area of life and fail in other
   areas
-Feel out of control of their lives
-Feel like all they ever do is manage crises
-Don't get what they want out of life
-Don't feel excited about their life
-Don't grow
-Aren't peaceful
-Don't have a sense of meaning or purpose in life

A great marriage is built of two equal partners that are each adequate and competent. They think for themselves and their actions are based on conscious direction. They can each handle the tasks of daily living.

Each partner was normally dependent to varying degrees during their childhood, gradually outgrowing the child's self-centeredness and inexperience, to become evermore able to relate to others in an emotionally healthy way and evermore competent. In out-growing dependence by living through it and mastering competence – rather than skipping it and pretending to be competent and mature when not in reality – each partner reaches a level of independence required to function at their best in the adult world.

However, independence is not the ultimate goal. Rather, interdependence is the mode of relatedness that comes from maturity. No man is an island. All of us live better when we can collaborate with others. The most competent and adequate person still needs others at times.

The mode of relatedness you are seeking in an effective partner is the ability to function interdependently. That means you are each able to competently handle the tasks of daily living. And it means that during times of high stress or illness that you can each lean on the other, temporarily. You are neither diminished nor crippled by temporary leaning or being leaned upon.

A great marriage doesn't just mean making it through the day. A great marriage means soaring through the day.

On the following pages describe your partner's effectiveness.

Describe Your Partner's Effectiveness

What does your partner say is important in life? Does he or she have a good job that they are happy doing?

_____

_____

_____

_____

_____

_____

_____

_____

_____

_____

_____

_____

_____

_____

_____

_____

_____

_____

_____

_____

What goals has your partner accomplished and what goals does he or she have for the future?

_____

_____

_____

_____

_____

_____

_____

_____

_____

_____

_____

_____

_____

_____

_____

_____

_____

_____

_____

_____

_____

_____

What in his or her life makes your partner lead a rich, rewarding, and balanced life?

_____

_____

_____

_____

_____

_____

_____

_____

_____

_____

_____

_____

_____

_____

_____

_____

_____

_____

_____

How well does your partner handle the tasks of daily living? Do they go to work regularly? Do they pay their bills on time? Do they live within their means? Do they feed themselves nourishing meals? Do they keep themselves healthy and fit? Do they keep their clothes clean and in good repair? Do they avoid addictive habits? Do they keep their car and home in good repair? Do they keep their living environment clean and orderly?

_____

_____

_____

_____

_____

_____

_____

_____

_____

_____

_____

_____

_____

_____

_____

_____

_____

Does Your Partner

Question	Yes	No
Have too much to do in too little time most of the time?		
Does your partner spend most of his or her time doing tasks that seem trivial – like lots of busywork?		
Succeed in one area of life and fail in other areas?		
Feel out of control of his or her life?		
Feel like all they ever do is manage crises?		
Get what they want out of life, consistently?		
Feel excited about his or her life?		
Demonstrate an effort to stretch and grow psychologically and intellectual?		
Experience peace?		
Have a sense of meaning or purpose in life?		

A "yes" answer to the first 5 questions and a "no" answer to the last 5 questions show ineffectiveness.

Score your partner from 1 (least effective) to 10 (most effective) for his or her effectiveness.

☐

To help objectify this as much as possible, we've asked you to score your partner's overall effectiveness. Your partner is operating effectively enough for marriage if his or her score is seven or above. A high score on effectiveness cannot balance a low score on one of the other questions. They must all be seven or above.

If ineffective, ask yourself why he or she isn't effective. Ask yourself if you want to be parental in your relationship to them.

Do they show signs of improving their effectiveness? How?

_____

_____

_____

_____

_____

_____

_____

_____

_____

_____

Our opinion is that anyone can improve his or her effectiveness given some effort and determination, but if your partner isn't effective, you're taking a gamble on something that hasn't happened yet and you cannot count on your partner changing. You should make your decision based on the here and now. If this partner isn't effective and you are effective, he or she will not be your equal. He or she can't be a perfect partner contributing to a great marriage.

Remember, marriage is for adults and when you bring yourself to the dating marketplace you need to be all of the things you want your partner to be. They need to be all they want you to be. If you marry someone that's ineffective you'll spend at least some of your time in a parental role and picking up the slack – or even worse – living a chaotic life.

If your partner is somewhat effective, you have a better chance, but all of the same applies. People do continue to mature. If they don't, you may be able to live with the amount of ineffectiveness they bring into your life, depending on how ineffective he or she is.

When you and your partner are highly effective, you have the makings of a great marriage with a high level of satisfaction. You can have a marriage where you will both contribute to the best you each can be and to the best a marriage can be.

Couple # 1's Answer to Question # 2

Gary's answer: Very – organized for the most part – very motivated – task completion type person. The only area she is not effective in her life is some relationships with family and me.

Gary's score for Susan = 5

Susan's answer: Susan didn't answer this question.

Susan's score = 0

Couple # 2's Answer to Question #2

Anne Marie's answer: Matthew can be very effective in the things he wants for himself. He can be very selfish at times also. He wants to be babied too much too!

Anne Marie's score = 5

Matthew's answer: ?

Matthew's score = 0

Our Comments

Susan's lack of response is most likely related to already feeling drained from her marriage and having reached a level of indifference. The indifference is not a good sign. Anger and rage evidence a continued emotional connection. Indifference is a lack of emotional connection.

Gary's response is blaming and critical, which,

when added to other comments he's made, indicate that he believes Susan is at fault. His tone is a bit condescending.

This couple's ineffectiveness is contributing negatively to their marriage. However, Susan's appearance of ineffectiveness may be mostly indifference. In any event, ineffectiveness inflicts further harm to this marriage.

Anne Marie's answer demonstrates that she's less than satisfied with her husband's level of effectiveness.

Matthew's lack of a response was supposedly because he didn't understand what we meant by effectiveness. When explored, he was able to conclude that he sees his wife as effective in some areas of her life, but not in other areas.

Anne Marie and Matthew's shared ineffectiveness is part of not having resolved past issues in their life and letting those issues become part of the marriage. Their role models for effectiveness were poor so they haven't learned important skills. Ineffectiveness is at the heart of this couple's problems.

Question 3: Does Your Partner have his or her head straight?

For those of you who've read our book, you'll remember that getting your head straight means knowing who you are, matching your behavior to who you are, and liking yourself.

The way you feel about yourself influences how you relate to every person and situation in your life. The way you feel about yourself affects how you think about and interpret events. The way you understand events in your environment filters through the way you feel about yourself. When you feel good about yourself you convey to others that you believe in yourself. When you feel good about yourself, getting others to believe in you is relatively easy. When you feel good about yourself you expect that good will happen to you. Your expectation of happy endings results in happy endings.

People that don't know themselves attune their behaviors to what others expect and they behave as extensions of others from whom they seek approval. They count what others think about what's important more than they count what they think about what's important. When you don't know who you are, how can you know with whom you should match on the 16 differences? How can you be effective?

If you know who you are, but act like someone else, what difference does it make that you know who you are? Acting like someone other than who you are will get you a life other than what you want and other than what's good for you. If you accommodate to others, think about the layers of resentment that will build over time. Can you live, or even like someone for whom you feel so much resentment?

Can you be effective when your actions reflect someone else's beliefs rather than your own? How can someone that molds their behaviors to others' opinions have control over his or her life? The most ironic thing of all is that, people that don't have control over their own life try to control everyone else's life. They do that to have a measure of predictability over their life, but it doesn't work.

And not only do you have to know yourself and behave like yourself, you must like yourself. How can someone else like you if you don't like you? Or if they did, how could you ever believe them? People with healthy ways of thinking become cautious about those that transmit signals that you should be cautious about them. People with healthy ways of thinking, effective people, don't want to slow themselves down to carry the load of someone that should be carrying their own load. How would you feel about yourself if you knew you were slowing others down? That would add to your not feeling good about yourself or thinking admirably about yourself. When there is something about yourself that you don't like, change it. First, think about whether the quality deserves to have you disapprove or whether it's a quality that's fine, but that someone else has told you is bad. Think for yourself. Is the quality really bad? If it is, change it. If it isn't, then stop feeling bad about it.

But liking yourself isn't arrogance. We need to make sure you can distinguish between people who genuinely like themselves and someone who has an inflated sense of self or arrogance.

People that like themselves:
-Don't have any need to control and manipulate
 others
-Quietly go about making their lives happy and
 satisfying
-Attract people that like them, too
-Attract positive experiences
-Have certain limits and boundaries
-Rarely have crises to manage
-Like to learn about others' ideas and beliefs
-Can relate to many different kinds of people
-Toot their own horn in a dignified way
-Are realistic about their strengths and limita-
 tions
-Don't waste their time trying to be all things to
 all people
-May critique the behavior and opinions of others
 to think ideas through for themselves, but
 don't have a need to make others into their own
 image
-Choose how to spend their time and with whom
-Make the most out of what they have
-Take responsibility for their lives, acting in
 accordance with their values
-Are fit and healthy
-Choose healthy relationships in which to be
 involved

People that don't like themselves:
-Use a variety of active and passive behaviors to
 manipulate and control others
-Attract people that don't like them
-Often defend an inner sense of inferiority with
 an air of superiority
-Feel humiliated by being less than perfect

-Fear and abhor any kind of criticism, including constructive criticism
-Criticize others, as well as themselves
-Have a low tolerance for mistakes
-Rarely take chances or try new things
-Are self-effacing
-Have low self-acceptance
-Depend on the opinion of others for their self-esteem; approval bolsters self-esteem (or pseudo self-esteem) temporarily; disapproval sends their self-esteem crashing to the bottom of the pit
-Sometimes have an inflated sense of what they can do and can't allow themselves to know what they don't know

The lists could go on, but you get the idea. Arrogance is the opposite of healthy self-esteem. In most cases superiority is a façade and demonstrates inferiority through the behavior of someone that thinks and acts as though they're better than others are. Of course, some people truly believe that they are better than others are. Someone that likes himself or herself is humble, but realistic about whom they are and what they can do.

If you have questions concerning self-esteem, read *The Six Pillars of Self-Esteem* by Nathaniel Branden (Bantam, 1994). Healthy self-esteem is the quality necessary for liking yourself. Healthy self-esteem means having a good reputation with yourself.

All of these ideas apply to your partner. Does your partner have his or her head straight?

Describe Your Partner

How well does your partner know himself or herself? What does he or she do that leads you to believe that they know themselves?

_____

_____

_____

_____

_____

_____

_____

_____

_____

_____

_____

_____

_____

_____

_____

_____

_____

_____

_____

_____

_____

_____

Describe how your partner matches his or her actions with what they believe and who they are.

_____

_____

_____

_____

_____

_____

_____

_____

_____

_____

_____

_____

_____

_____

_____

_____

_____

_____

_____

_____

_____

_____

Describe how your partner demonstrates that they like themselves.

_____

_____

_____

_____

_____

_____

_____

_____

_____

_____

_____

_____

_____

_____

_____

_____

_____

_____

Score your partner 1 (don't have their head together) to 10 (do have their head together)

Couple #1's Answers to Question #3

Gary's answer: Susan hasn't gotten her head straight completely. She's still dealing with emotional baggage from her family. She's never really been out on her own, therefore doesn't realize how much she relies on and demands from others (closest to her). Also, we are (does he really mean, "she is"?) very much self focused.

Gary's score for Susan = 3

Susan's answer: No answer.

Susan's score for Gary = 0

Couple #2's Answer to Question #3

Anne Marie's answer: No. I feel Matthew is very stressed from work and brings it home too much – taking it out on the children and me. Plus his father and him and his brother have caused him plenty of problems. And he lets his daughter take advantage (makes him feel guilty) about not being around for her – he divorced when she was 2 years old. He spends too much money on her. And we argue about how she continues to take advantage. She is 21 years old. I feel he loves and cares for her more than our kids and me.

Anne Marie's score for Matthew = 3

Matthew's answer: No. Anne Marie has many problems from the past that effect our present relationship.

Matthew's score for Anne Marie = 3

Our Comments

Both couples need more guidance and exploration about exactly what constitutes having your head straight.

Again, Susan has given up. She doesn't have any energy to put into this exercise.

Gary gave himself away when he said "we" are too self-focused. His tone continues to convey a parental and condescending attitude toward Susan.

Anne Marie is invested and energetic in thinking through this answer and has some specific information that's useful. The issues she raises can be worked out if Matthew is open to doing so.

Matthew isn't specific, but is fully aware that Anne Marie's unfinished business is intruding on their marriage. But he doesn't sound blaming or scolding. Matthew continues to show warmth, concern, and tenderness toward his wife. He demonstrates a willingness to work their issues through.

It's easy to see why Gary and Susan ended up married to each other. They didn't know themselves or each other very well. And when they ran into differences they either blew them off (Susan) or made an ongoing major case in complaints (Gary). They both need to get their head straight and this issue is adding more stress to their incompatibility.

Anne Marie and Matthew have more adequate coping skills, know and like themselves better, and are less defensive about facing the truth. They demonstrate a ready ability to explore their issues and desire to try new behaviors.

Do you need to work on getting your head straight? Does your partner need to work on getting their head straight? What exactly do each of you need to work on?

_____

_____

_____

_____

_____

_____

_____

_____

_____

_____

_____

_____

_____

_____

_____

_____

_____

_____

If you or your partner needs to work on getting your head straight and you'd like more guidance, please see our book, *Perfect Partners™: Make Your Hopes and Dreams for a Great Marriage Come True* or our workbook, *Perfect Partners™: Find Your Perfect Partner Step-By-Step.*

Question 4: Is your partner genuine, honest, and trustworthy? Do they have character and integrity?

All the fame and fortune in the world cannot equal the true love of a faithful perfect partner.

Is your partner faithful?

The qualities that we will discuss here are necessary for a high level of adult function; the level of function that a great marriage requires.

Genuineness

Someone who is genuine tells you who he or she really is with his or her words and behavior. Their talk and deeds are filled with sincerity and match. They don't put on airs. They don't wear masks. They're not phony. They don't hide themselves from you. When they tell you how they feel you can believe them. Being genuine means living honestly. They don't say they aren't angry with you with clenched fists and jaw. They don't con you with empty compliments. They don't charm you just to get their way.

Your perfect partner is genuine.

Honesty

Honest people tell the truth and live the truth. Some people are dishonest unintentionally and some people are dishonest intentionally. Neither can have a great marriage. Honest people are worthy of trust. Dishonest people, whether dishonest intentionally or unintentionally, cannot be trusted.

Your perfect partner is honest.

Trustworthy

Have you ever been blamed for not trusting others? Some people believe that there is something wrong with someone that doesn't trust someone else. It's true that some people have been harmed psychologically and have difficulty trusting others even if they may be worthy of trust. With some work with trustworthy people these people can repair their inability to trust. But most people have the capacity to trust others. When those people don't trust someone it's important for them to listen to themselves so something bad doesn't happen to them.

The point that those people who accuse you or others of not trusting them or someone else misses is that someone must be worthy of trust if you are to trust them. Isn't it terribly foolish to trust someone that isn't worthy of trust just to give them the benefit of the doubt?

On the other hand, sometimes when a person cannot trust others they are projecting onto the other person. What that means is that since they themselves cannot be trusted they believe that no one else can be trusted.

In any case, you must pay attention and live through enough experiences with someone to determine whether or not they are worthy of trust.

And you should make a conscious decision about whether to trust someone not blindly trust others.

You can trust perfect partners and they can trust you.

Character

A person with character has moral and ethical strength. J.C. Watts, Rep. from Oklahoma, says, "character is doing what's right when no one is looking." Living by guiding principles helps us do what is right and helps us respect others and ourselves.

Developing a conscience assists with moral and ethical strength. Many people do what is right because they're afraid they'll get caught. People with character do what is right just because it feels better – they like themselves when they do what's right.

Your perfect partner has character.

Integrity

Someone with integrity lives up to his or her principles and values. They don't compromise and negotiate something they believe is right or wrong. Someone with integrity doesn't abandon their values and principles because someone else teases them or disapproves of them. They don't say one thing and do another.

Perfect partners have integrity.

Each one of these qualities works with the others. It's difficult to separate them, but each also has subtle qualities of its own. Your partner having or not having these qualities can mean the difference between a poor marriage, a marriage of convenience, and a great marriage. Partners having these qualities add more positive energy to your relationship. When your partner has these qualities, you won't have to spend your time and energy on managing crises, losses, and emotional pain as a regular part of your relationship.

Perfect partners are genuine, honest, trustworthy, and they have character and integrity.

What does your partner say and do that leads you
to believe that he or she is genuine?

_____

_____

_____

_____

_____

_____

_____

_____

_____

_____

_____

_____

_____

_____

_____

_____

_____

_____

_____

_____

_____

What does your partner say and do that leads you to believe that he or she is honest?

_____

_____

_____

_____

_____

_____

_____

_____

_____

_____

_____

_____

_____

_____

_____

_____

_____

_____

_____

_____

_____

_____

_____

What does your partner say and do that leads you to believe that he or she is worthy of your trust?

_____

_____

_____

_____

_____

_____

_____

_____

_____

_____

_____

_____

_____

_____

_____

_____

_____

_____

_____

_____

_____

_____

What does your partner say and do that demonstrates character?

_____

_____

_____

_____

_____

_____

_____

_____

_____

_____

_____

_____

_____

_____

_____

_____

_____

_____

_____

_____

_____

_____

_____

_____

What does your partner say and do that demon-strates integrity?

_____

_____

_____

_____

_____

_____

_____

_____

_____

_____

_____

_____

_____

_____

_____

_____

_____

Score your partner from 1 (least qualities listed) to 10 (most qualities listed)

Couple #1's Answers to Question #4

Gary's answer: Exceptional – except not always with me – we both tell small white lies. She has good integrity.

Gary's score for Susan = 8

Susan's answer: No answer.

Susan's score for Gary = 0

Couple #2's Answer to Question #4

Anne Marie's answer: Sometimes I feel Matthew isn't trustworthy – I have confided in him about my past marriage and upbringing and other issues. When we're arguing, he uses them against me.

Anne Marie's score for Matthew = 5

Matthew's answer: I don't have much trust in Anne Marie. She uses things I say to her in trust against me when we argue. She doesn't do what she promises.

Matthew's score for Anne Marie = 3

Our Comments

Neither couple gives us much information to go by. With these answers and what they've each said before, we can recognize the difficulty they each have in trusting the other. Lack of trust on Gary and Susan's part is largely due to "little white lies" and personal attacks. Lack of trust on Anne Marie and Matthew's is due to dirty fighting.

People tell lies when they feel they must protect themselves. When your relationship lacks emotional safety you feel you must protect yourself. The inability to act with integrity – dishonestly – by being someone you're not – by telling lies – prevents intimacy. Intimacy is the act of self-disclosure. Gary and Susan must answer this entire question in the negative.

Dirty fighting prevents conflict resolution, prevents win-win in your marriage, and erodes trust. Dirty fighting includes any form of intimidation, dredging up old hurts or past trespasses, name calling, and blaming the other person for the entire disagreement. When either marriage partner loses, both partners lose. Conflict resolution in marriage must result in both partners winning.

Anne Marie and Matthew are eroding the trust they have with each other. They must stop or they'll eventually cash in all of their chips.

Question 5: Is there some magic? Are you attracted to each other?

Most people base their belief that they've found the right partner on chemistry and physical attraction. They believe that if you have plenty of chemistry it must mean love and that they've found the right partner.

It doesn't work that way. Physical attraction – chemistry – is important, but you can't make it the first and only thing on which you base your selection. A relationship based mostly on physical chemistry won't last because sooner or later someone more attractive will come along. If you want a great marriage rather than a poor marriage or a marriage of convenience, you can't base your choice of partner just on magic.

We've deliberately made this question last because only having magic isn't enough and too many people believe that it's the primary factor. But being physically attracted is the icing on the cake not the cake. If you can't answer the four previous questions affirmatively, no matter how much chemistry you have you'll never have a great marriage. You'll have another one of those marriages that you'll have to work very hard at to make it work or you'll, at best, live largely separate lives with parallel play – a marriage of convenience.

You can and will be attracted to many more people in this world than your partner. Noticing the attraction makes you feel good, but making a commitment to your partner means not following though on the attraction. And being attracted doesn't mean you match on the 16 differences that make a difference or that the other three questions have affirmative answers.

On the other hand, someone with whom you match very well and you can answer the three other questions in the affirmative can build some magic with you over time that just gets stronger and stronger as time goes by.

If everything else looks good for this to be your perfect partner, then if you have some excitement to begin with – even at the level of looking forward to having a fun and interesting time with them – the chances are that magic will follow quickly behind. Feeling instant intense physical attraction is far more likely to blind you to other problems in the relationship than to indicate that you've found your perfect partner.

Doesn't it make sense to you that spending time with someone that's interesting and mature and that has compatible values can develop an intensifying attraction as you build a history together? Magic with the right partner deepens and intensifies over time. Your attunement and the supportive climate for being who you really are sparks magic, electricity, and energy. Magic with the wrong partner can leave as suddenly as it came.

There isn't much to answering this question – a yes or no answer tells it all.

Are you physically attracted to your partner? Is there some magic?

Yes ?   ☐

No ?   ☐

Do you think that more attraction and chemistry will develop over time?

Yes ?   ☐

No ?   ☐

Score 1 (least) to 10 (most)

☐

Couple #1's Answer to Question #5

Gary's answer: I am physically attracted to Susan, but there isn't much magic anymore.

Gary's score for his attraction to Susan = 7

Susan's answer: Yes, I'm physically attracted to Gary.

Susan's score for her attraction to Gary = 5

Couple #2's Answer to Question #5

Anne Marie's answer: Yes, except for when I'm angry at him, which is more lately than ever. I want to stay completely away from him! Sometimes looking at him makes me sick and yet I feel he can be handsome also!

Anne Marie's score for her attraction to Matthew = 8

Matthew's answer: I do feel attracted to Anne Marie, but I don't think she finds me attractive. There isn't much magic now, but there was....

Matthew's score for his attraction to Anne Marie = 8

Our Comment

When Carolyn explored this issue further with Gary and Susan, she learned that, while they felt attracted to each other, neither had ever felt much magic. The most Carolyn could get them to admit to was a sense of missing each other when they were apart. The tone of their relationship was convenience and the lifestyle they could have together, not chemistry. Sometimes, when all else fails, sexual attraction can be the glue, but not in this marriage.

As Susan realized how incompatible she and Gary are, and how she and Gary need desperately to improve their relationship skills, she questioned why in the world they ever ended up together in the first place. Susan realized that on several occasions they'd almost ended the relationship. They had even postponed their wedding. Each time they returned to each other with little resolution of their problems. They just went on from there. Susan returned because she was drawn to the idea of the lifestyle they'd be able to live on their incomes. Gary seems to have returned out of convenience.

Gary and Susan keep trying to make it. Gary says Susan doesn't try hard enough. Our prognosis is poor. Our recommendation is to end the marriage. They must also, each resolve their own unfinished business and master better relationship skills, or we predict that they'll find new – familiar – partners and carry on where they left off.

Anne Marie and Matthew generate electricity in their therapy sessions. Their eyes brighten and their faces light up when they talk about each other and what they had in the beginning. Talking about how wonderful it was is almost enough to pull them through.

Anne Marie and Matthew are each other's perfect partners. They're not perfect, but very close. Close enough that they should resolve their unfinished business and master better relationship skills.

These five crucial questions helped both couples discern whether their problems were related to incompatibility or relationship skills. It's fairly clear that Gary and Susan have low compatibility and poor relationship skills. Anne Marie and Matthew have higher compatibility, but have two areas in particular, of poor relationship skills.

We haven't tried to define an overall score that demonstrates the ability to "make it". Use the scores on the last four questions to clarify the extent to which you each need to work on relationship skills. If you have a high level of compatibility, work hard on those relationship skills and fight for your marriage. If you have a low level of compatibility, we recommend you leave and give everyone the opportunity for happiness. You will still need to work on having the best relationship skills possible so that your next relationship – with your perfect partner – will be all that it can be.

We hope the examples we've given you of Gary and Susan and Anne Marie and Matthew help you understand what you must do with these exercises. Let us caution you, that, due to space and the nature of the way each couple's story unfolds in therapy, these stories are short. Without the benefit of therapy and the exploration that comes with it, you'll need to make sure you give complete, well thought out answers in order to learn what you must learn. Short cuts won't work. Take your time and give detailed answers.

Benjamin found his perfect partner...
Both of the couples from our above examples came

into therapy because their marriages were in trouble. Their answers reflect that. We want you to have an example of answers from someone who has truly found his perfect partner to see how well perfect partners match. The following example is a man in his 40's. His name is Benjamin (changed to protect his identity).

Question #1
Benjamin: Sex makes me feel loved and I can't think of a better way of connecting with your partner. I like to make love at least once a day, even better would be twice a day. Life makes it hard to have sex often, but I think it's top priority to maintain a close bond with your wife. I like some adventure, nothing inappropriate. I especially like to see my partner's body. I'm very visual and looking at my partner and erotic movies is a real turn on. I'm affectionate. I like to hold hands and cuddle in front of the TV or a fire. I like to show my affection to my partner and I like her to be affectionate toward me. I think it's healthy for your children to know you love each other. Tasteful displays of affection in front of them are good for them. What could make your children feel safer than knowing their mom and dad really like and love each other?

I made a serious mistake in my last marriage by marrying someone that didn't like sex very much. Sex ended up being a weapon she used against me. Unfortunately, she didn't show me the real her until after we were married and our marriage went steadily downhill after having two children. Within two years of having our second child she said she wanted a divorce. Sometimes I think she just used me to have children. This time I knew I wanted to be with someone that loves me and likes sex as much as I do. I want to be with someone who

enjoys her adult sexuality. I want to be with someone who isn't afraid to be honest about who they
are.

My partner loves to make love almost everyday. She
isn't shy about letting me look at her and even if
she doesn't feel like making love she is always willing to satisfy me. Quickies are fun for us. I love to
make love with her. One of the things I like the
most is how safe I feel with her. In my last marriage
my sexual performance really suffered after a
while. It's hard to be sexy when you feel resentment and hatred from your partner. It's hard to be
sexy when you're shamed and criticized most of
the time. I even started having symptoms of heart
disease that curbed my sexual ability. All of those
symptoms are gone now that I'm in better shape
and with the right partner. I never have any trouble
with sexual performance.

Sex is so emotionally and physically satisfying
because I feel important to my partner and I know
I'm satisfying her because she's so genuine and
honest with me about how she feels. We can talk
about anything.

Score = 10

I am 44 and my partner is 44.

I have become extremely health conscious. Health
and fitness became an issue in my first marriage,
even though they weren't an issue at the beginning
of our marriage. I have never smoked nor drunk
alcohol. I've never used drugs. I used to eat terribly
and get moderate exercise.

My first wife's smoking, in particular, became a

source of conflict. She never went out, so she did her drinking at home. Drinking wasn't as much of a problem as the smoking.

Now I still don't smoke and drink, but I watch my diet, eat healthy food and exercise routinely. My health is much better than it used to be. I used to have problems with chest pain, palpitations, and impotence, but I don't have any of those problems anymore. Between eating and exercising better and having a much better relationship, I'm much healthier with no signs of cardiovascular disease at all.

My partner used to smoke and drink alcohol, but she's stopped both because she wanted to be healthy. She stopped smoking many years ago, but only recently stopped most alcohol intake when she had increasing difficulty keeping her weight down. Too many empty calories and alcohol took all of her energy away. She eats as health consciously as she can, but can't eat some things because of allergies. She exercises regularly. We match very well on health and fitness issues.

Score = 10

The climate didn't matter as much to me in the past as it does now. I'm getting tired of winter and not being able to go outside for weeks in the summer because it's too hot and humid to do anything.

I like to live in a neighborhood that seems somewhat private, but is still close to shopping areas. When I retire I'd like to live somewhere the weather is good most of the time. If it were too hot in the summer I'd like to travel then to cooler regions.

As I've become more aware of the effect politics has on daily life, I've also become more aware of living in a state that has politics I can live with.

My partner thinks the same as I do about where to live with a couple of exceptions. She prefers the south to the West Coast because of politics and the type of natural disasters the west is prone to, namely, earthquakes and fires. She also doesn't like the desert. She also has allergies that make certain areas more comfortable than others. I don't think where we live will ever be an issue because we have enough in common to have many choices we could both live with.

Score = 9

I have a master's degree in math and science and an MBA. When I was looking for my current partner, I knew I wanted someone who was interested in what I was interested in. I can remember dating women who I was very sexually attracted to, but I had almost nothing to say to them.

My partner has a master's degree in a health science. She likes technology and science in a more practical sense, but we each know enough about each other's area to have intelligent conversations about what we do. We have many common interests and never have any problem finding things to talk about.

In my first marriage my wife didn't have any interest in what I did and I wasn't interested in much of what she did. We didn't have much to talk about. Our differences in this area may not have caused our divorce, but it certainly didn't contribute anything positive. If we'd had more to talk about and more interest in each other's lives maybe we could have overcome some of our other shortcomings. I never dreamed that my wife wouldn't be my friend and have an interest in what I spent the day doing. And the same with me for her. It's very lonely not being interested in your marriage partner and her not being interested in you.

This time my partner and I have an active interest in what each of us does and in what interest the other. So much mutual interest is energizing and validating.

Score = 10

I like a casual lifestyle. I like to camp, hike, bike, and walk around the house in my shorts and bare feet or slippers. I enjoy TV, good fiction, and movies. I like all kinds of movies from action oriented to romantic.

My partner is just like me. She walks around in shorts and flip-flops, like's to be outside in nature, hike, bike and while she doesn't like the idea of tent camping, she is very enthusiastic about an RV and traveling. We both love the same kind of movies. We always have so much we can do together. Even when we're home doing different things we're usually in the same room. We're both clutterbugs, too. As long as the house is clean, we're fine, even with piles of our things around. We're so busy with the projects we're working on we don't have time to be worried about clutter.

My first wife drove me crazy. She only thought that we should do everything her way and that any other way was bad. Not just different, but bad. We had very separate lives and she was always nagging me to pick up and do cultural things with her. It was like I was from outer space to her, because I didn't like everything she liked.

It feels really nice to be with someone that is comfortable with me the way I am. Actually, it feels great! What a relief.

Score = 10

Right after college I thought that I'd like the lifestyle of teaching. But I had trouble with the politics of getting a Ph.D. and didn't get along with some of the faculty. I just couldn't make it and became very disappointed in myself when I couldn't do it. Then I tried teaching at the high school level and didn't like that at all. My whole idea of what I wanted to do for a living changed drastically within a year or two of graduating. I ended up getting a job in industry and I liked the design work I got to do on some very important projects. I don't particularly like office politics, but I have liked working on the things I've done. And my employer even put me through a good MBA program and I like seeing the business angle of the design work I do. Anyway, my career has turned out differently than I expected, but I liked most of it. My ex-wife really hated the changes.

When I am at work, I focus on getting the right things done, not working endless hours. I think that a balance between work and family is extremely important. I see people at work who work late at night, every night, and I think to myself that they must not have any family life.

Now, I'm feeling as though I need to work for myself. And I realize that my thinking is even more innovative that imagined. The idea of really making a difference in the world because of what work I do appeals to me very much. My partner and I both want to work for ourselves, so we've designed a plan to do so one at a time. We'd both like to contribute positively to the world. What we're working on is exciting and energizing.

We'd both like to put our effort into the projects we've been working on, make as much money as we can, and retire early. After retirement we'd like to work behind the scenes for the political candidates that we like.

Score = 10

I'm very conscious about money issues because money became such a bone of contention in my first marriage. Money issues were a serious problem for my partner in her first marriage. So we've talked about money to make sure we have similar ideas.

When I got married to my first wife, we had no idea how much everything cost. We didn't know how much it would cost to raise children. We didn't even talk about money. I guess we just thought it would sort of take care of itself. Now that I look back on my life in my first marriage I'm convinced that my ex-wife didn't think we'd be together for retirement so she couldn't care less about planning for it. She wanted out of the marriage so she just wanted money to spend while she was there. Whenever I talked or planned for retirement income she became irate about it because she believed we should spend it now.
Now that I've come to realize just how much money it takes to live and I've become awakened to how

much freedom it can give you, we plan accordingly. My partner and I think exactly the same about money. There is nothing inherently wrong with money. Having it and earning it doesn't take it away from anyone else. The more competent you are at living and earning the more freedom you have and the more you can spend in the marketplace. Every dollar you spend in the marketplace gives other people jobs. Everyone is helped when there is a free flow of money. Money is an exchange for energy. We both take responsibility to save and invest for our retirement. We both like to live comfortably and to be able to travel. We both would like to continue to enjoy a comfortable retirement. We feel responsible for making it happen for ourselves.

We also both feel trapped when working for others. We make the money for others to pocket and don't get much influence in the decision making about products. We're both innovative and free spirits and want to be financially independent.

We both agree that the children deserve to have a helping hand to get their primary college degrees and then they are on their own.

Score = 10

I want my wife to have a good job and be financially successful so that I can put my kids through school.

I didn't realize when I was younger how important it is to spend time with each other. I tried hard to get my first wife to do things together, but she didn't very much. I guess I just sort of went my own way. That's the way many marriages are, so, even though I was lonely, I guess I just suffered.

Now that I have this relationship I can see how important friendship is to marriage. In my first marriage we didn't have much in common, our view of life was very different, and we had no friendship.

I want my marriage to give me my best friend and nurturing, supportive companionship. I want to talk to my wife about everything and I want her to talk to me about everything. Isn't that what intimacy is all about. My first marriage was just a convenience for my wife to have children. I want a real relationship.

My partner is my best friend and I am her best friend. Neither of us would rather do things with others, we both have the most fun with each other. Nothing compares to the emotional safety and support we've found with each other. It's like heaven on earth and we don't have to work at it at all. It just comes naturally.

Score = 10

A healthy and attractive body is important to me. The body build doesn't matter to me much except for the fitness. Tall or short doesn't matter much. But I do really like dark-haired women with pale skin. I can still remember one of the first girls I ever saw without her clothes. She had very pale skin and dark hair. Beautiful.

My partner works at keeping healthy and fit. She has to watch her weight and work out to keep from gaining, but she has a good body. She has dark hair and pale skin. She used to tan herself, but she stopped when she realized how damaging it was to her skin. And I like her skin pale so I think she looks terrific. My partner is attracted to me also.

She actually likes bald men.

Score = 10

My parents made me go to Sunday school and church like most parents did when I was growing up. Organized religion seemed hypocritical to me. I saw so much hypocrisy everywhere I turned. I still do. I'm not sure if I believe in God. I'm a little iffy on that. Generally, I think if you're going to make extraordinary claims like the existence of God you better have good support for the claim. But I do believe that abiding by Christian principles is the right way to live. Christian principles give us a framework by which to live that works for everyone. I practice Christian principles in my daily living. You don't have to go to church to practice Christian principles. Going to church doesn't necessarily mean you live by Christian principles.

My partner believes adamantly in God. She does, however, also dislike organized religion for the same reasons as I. My partner has had a near-death experience and some other experiences that have convinced her of a greater power. She didn't send her children to church or Sunday school, but they went with friends from time to time. Her children were raised by Christian principles. My partner believes that spirituality is a personal experience that each soul reconnects with as they evolve through the human experience. She doesn't have any problem with my position of skepticism because she believes that living by the guiding principles of Christianity is what counts. She believes that we all go through stages of doubt and wonder and that each of our souls evolves through a process of individuation and becoming who we are to reconnect with the one greater power of which we are all a part. She says you can't skip steps and the resolution of doubt comes as a personal experience when that individuation has taken place.

Score = 10

When I was younger I didn't really know the difference between political parties. Politics has become much more important to me as I've realized how much the decisions and policies of the government affect our lives. When I met my first wife I really didn't know much. Over the years, as I worked more in the world and life's issues like how to pay for everything and raise children, came to the forefront, I began to have strong views in opposition to what my ex-wife believed. Over the years of our marriage we grew further apart because my ideas changed profoundly and her ideas didn't change. I don't know how we could have known any better unless we would have waited to get married until we knew ourselves better in relation to work and adult responsibilities.

My partner and I have very similar views about politics and the effect that the government has on our lives. We're actively interested in politics and we keep a dialogue going with our representatives so they stay current with our views. Both of us realize that our political beliefs are grounded in values that we have and feel adamant about participating in the political process. We'd both like to volunteer some of our time to the candidates of our choice when we retire. We're supportive of them now.

Score = 10

It was just sort of unspoken knowledge that I'd

have children when I got married the first time. We never discussed the topic before marriage, but I thought it would be okay to have children. We agreed to have the first child and then we agreed later to have the second child. At least I got to be involved in the decision making about having them. I never got much influence in what they did from day-to-day. My ex-wife disagreed on how to prepare children for their adult lives. She was extremely permissive. I wanted to provide more structure and limits in keeping with the way the world works. As a result our children were caught in the middle or our disagreement. Because my ex-wife withheld sex from me if I didn't go along with her, I learned to keep quiet about most things. I shouldn't have. I should have spoken up any way. Keeping quiet never solved anything. In fact it made matters worse. It didn't get my children's needs nor my own met.

Thank God my partner and I agree on how to raise children. In fact, my partner has raised very competent and successful children and she's helped me a lot in catching up with my one child. It's beginning to look like the relationship I have with my daughter will never be repaired. I feel badly for her because our dysfunctional relationship affects every area of her life – especially her relationship with men. Children shouldn't have to pay for their parents' mistakes.

My partner and I have both had children in previous marriages. We don't want to have any more. Four out of the five have graduated from college and we're both ready for some freedom to do what we want. Neither of us even wants a pet at this point. Importantly, we both have the same degree of a sense of responsibility to our children. We agree on offering the kind of support they need to begin adult lives of their own. We agree on providing the best basic college possible given the amount of money we have to spend. We both agree that children need to be on their own when they finish a basic college degree. If they return for graduate degrees they'll be on their own. We both agree on how to help children become competent so they can take their adult places in the world and be the best they can be.

In my first marriage my ex-wife and I disagreed on how to raise children. My first child had a habit of going to her mother every time she didn't like what I wanted her to do – which was most of the time. My ex-wife would then scold me unmercifully which decreased my credibility with my children. As our marriage fell apart and my ex-wife built more and more resentment and I felt more and more pushed aside, my relationship with one of my children really suffered. The anger her mother had at me became my daughter's way of relating to me, too. I think it got even worse because my ex-wife couldn't stand conflict so she pretended like things were okay even when they weren't. Finally she'd blow up. But my daughter's relationship with me is permeated with anger. It's one of the saddest things I've ever seen in my life – what a bad marriage can do to children is forever and very painful.

Another thing that was destructive to my first marriage was my ex-wife's over-involvement with the children. They became her whole life and her relationship with me was non-existent. Not only did it deprive me of any relationship, but also my children were kept dependent on their mother far too long. Fortunately, we've been able to help my second child feel less guilty for growing up.

Score = 10

I'm very settled into my career as is my partner. We'll both be making a shift to owning our own company and working for ourselves. We'll make the shift one at a time so we can have the stability of a paycheck while my partner gets the company going. As soon as the company has enough income I'll make the switch. Career and work wise we're in the same place. I still have one child to finish high school and college. My partner's children are all college graduates, married, and on their own. We're a little out of synch there, but it's minor and helps us rather than hurts us. We only have one to go.

In my first marriage we were mostly in synch life stage wise, but my ex-wife resented having to go to work before I did to support us while I finished an advanced degree. Otherwise, we were okay on this score.

Score = 10

I like to work and play on my computer at times and I like a mixture of outdoor and indoor activities during my leisure. I like to watch TV and channel surf often watching more than one program at a time. I like to go to movies – all kinds. I like to travel. I like to read at times. I also like to ride my bike and do some light hiking. I like to do those things with my partner rather than alone.
My partner likes to do the same kinds of things I like to do. She doesn't watch TV much, but usually sits with me and reads or works on something in the same room. She likes to balance active and passive activity. We love movies and like the same kinds. We like to go out to eat. We're best friends and would rather do most things with each other.

We have more fun with each other than we have with anyone else.

Doing leisure with my best friend is great. My first marriage was very lonely. My ex-wife wouldn't do anything with me. Not doing things together certainly didn't help us foster intimacy and a history together. Our bond was considerably lessened because of it.

Score = 10

I usually have plenty of energy. I'm not always up and doing something physical. I like to have some passive activity. I also spend a lot of time thinking and have quite a bit of mental energy.

My partner is slightly more energetic than I am. She has a balance of mental and physical energy and likes a balance of active and passive activities.

I'm definitely a morning person and so is my partner.

Score = 9

Benjamin and his partner

Differences that Make a Difference	Score
Sex drives/sexual interests/ demonstrations of affection	10
Age	10
Health & Fitness, including smoking, drinking, and/or using drugs	10
Where to live	9
Education/Intelligence	10
Lifestyle	10
Views about work/Level of ambition	10
Views on how to handle and spend money	10
Expectations of marriage/relationship	10
Physical characteristics attractive to you	10
Religion	10
Politics	10
Children (has or wants)	10
Life stage	10
Common leisure interests	10
Energy levels	9

Total=   **158**

Benjamin's Answer to Question #2

What does your partner say is important in life?
She would say loving and being loved; a great marriage; the right partner; marrying someone you can like, admire, be loyal to, and feel affection for; having the qualities you want your partner to have; living as honestly as you can; taking responsibility for what you say and do; living on purpose and in the here and now; doing work you love; helping others help themselves; people rather than things; offering yourself and others emotional safety; being the best you can be; honoring self and others; investing belief in your children; loving your children and letting them go; believing in yourself and others; being open to new experiences; having character and integrity; justice; good over evil; balancing work you love with fun and relaxation; health and fitness; connecting with nature, learning from your mistakes and moving on; to risk living fully engaged in life; and having and living your spiritual beliefs are important in life.

What goals has your partner accomplished and what goals does he or she have for the future?
She has overcome many psychological barriers she had from growing up in a dysfunctional family. She has committed to living what she believes is important in life and is largely successful in doing so. She successfully raised three wonderful children against all odds. She continuously re-evaluates her goals and she replaces accomplished goals with new goals.

What in his or her life makes your partner lead a rich, rewarding, and balanced life?
She constantly seeks to grow and stretch herself. She spends reflective time learning what she can

about herself and her behavior. She lives her life based on what she believes is important. She has a questioning mind and avoids living on automatic pilot. She's healthy. She's fully engaged in life. She's found the right marriage partner after much emotional pain and with great determination. She has a sense of direction and purpose. She refuses to limit herself to what's been before. She spends most of her time exposing herself to healthy and nurturing people and experiences, devoting time to toxic circumstances and people selectively and only when she feels strong and centered. She loves me.

How well does your partner handle the tasks of daily living? Do they go to work regularly? Do they pay their bills on time? Do they live within their means? Do they feed themselves nourishing meals? Do they keep themselves healthy and fit? Do they keep their clothes clean and in good repair? Do they avoid addictive habits? Do they keep their car and home in good repair? Do they keep their living environment clean and orderly?

My partner manages tasks of daily living very well. She does work she loves on a regular basis and responsibly. She has learned to manage money well. She is health and fitness conscious. Her appearance is excellent. She's had some addictions on and off in her life, but has given them up when she decided that she didn't want to be controlled by a substance. She keeps her possessions in good repair. She keeps her living environment clean and organized, but doesn't dwell on tidiness. She can be messy at time because she's so busy doing things. Underneath the clutter it's clean.

Does Your Partner

Question	Yes	No	I Don't Know
Have too much to do in too little time most of the time?		x	
Does your partner spend most of his or her time doing tasks that seem trivial – like lots of busywork?		x	
Succeed in one area of life and fail in other areas?		x	
Feel out of control of his or her life?		x	
Feel like all they ever do is manage crises?		x	
Get what they want out of life, consistently?	x		
Feel excited about his or her life?	x		
Demonstrate an effort to stretch and grow psychologically and intellectually?	x		
Experience peace?	x		
Have a sense of meaning or purpose in life?	x		

Give your partner a score between 1 (least effective) and 10 (most effective).

Score = 9.5   (Almost perfect, but still human)

Benjamin's answer to question #3

How well does your partner know himself or herself? What does he or she do that leads you to believe that they know themselves?
I don't have any trouble knowing about my partner in regard to the sixteen differences or about her effectiveness. I think that's true because she knows herself well so she doesn't have any trouble transmitting who she is to others.

Describe how your partner matches his or her actions with what they believe and who they are.
I never think of my partner as hypocritical. Her actions fit her words and beliefs. Her whole life is a reflection of who she is and she's aware of it. My partner contemplates about herself, her behavior, her feelings and thoughts, how her behavior affects her relationships, and a variety of other things. Her actions are rarely reactive; they're mostly purposeful actions after she has given some thought to the circumstances.

Describe how your partner demonstrates that they like themselves.
My partner shows that she likes herself in many different ways. She sets limits and boundaries. She does work that she likes to do. She relates to most other people. The only people that I've ever seen that don't relate well to her are people that have something to hide and that are uncomfortable with her openness and honesty. If she doesn't like being around someone she just leaves them alone. She keeps healthy and fit, but not fanatic. She has fun. She has plenty of love to give to others. She expects the best from life. She can give her opinion when appropriate. She can fight for what she believes. She manages her life without many crises

and seems at peace most of the time. She likes the way she looks and takes care of her appearance. When she slips a little, it doesn't take her long to get going again – with her diet, exercise, and fitness. She avoids unhealthy behaviors and habit. She chooses to be around pleasant and positive people but can help others in negative circumstances by staying centered and objective. She doesn't fall apart over much of anything. She accepts compliments graciously. She never hesitates to give compliments when warranted.

Benjamin's answer to question #4

What does your partner say and do that leads you to believe that he or she is genuine?
When she talks to others or me, she meets my eye easily. When we talk about something, she pays attention to what I'm saying and when she talks, she continues to concentrate and pay close attention. She gives me feedback about what I say that lets me know she understands what I'm saying. When I have trouble understanding what she's saying, she takes time and care to make sure I get what she means. Her behavior fits what she says.

What does your partner say and do that leads you to believe that he or she is honest?
What she says matches what happens. She doesn't say one thing and do another. She tells it like it is. When what she has to say is difficult, she says it anyway while trying to be tactful and diplomatic. If someone tries to talk her out of her beliefs or position, she listens and considers what they say and then she maintains her position if she still believes she's right. She doesn't lie to people just to buy their friendship or approval. She doesn't change

her mind when the audience changes.

What you see is what you get.

What does your partner say and do that leads you to believe that he or she is worthy of your trust?
By being honest and genuine my partner sometimes angers others and holds them accountable, but you can't trust and respect someone that adjusts their opinion for the audience and approval. She may stir up some controversy, but you know right where she stands and you can trust her because of that.
Also, she follows through on what she says she'll do. I can believe what she says. She keeps her word. She's open and talks over anything relevant to our lives. She's honest and sincere.

I can trust her because she never puts me down or ridicules me in private or with others present. She doesn't try to control me with shame. She genuinely likes me and shows it.

She doesn't change her mind with the whim of others. Her opinions are based in thoughtful consideration and fact. Few things trigger a reactive emotional response from her. (When someone discredits her or discounts her with little consideration for what she's said, she can show some temper and impatience. But she knows that being misunderstood, minimized, or discredited is an issue for her related to her past and she works consciously to let her intellect control her response rather than uncontrolled emotions). I can trust her to think things over and give me honest and friendly feedback. She can back up her ideas and beliefs with reasons. She never expects others or me to accept what she says just because she says it. She's willing to spend some time talking her ideas over and provide me with reasons and rationale. I can tell that she really thinks things through before she forms her opinion. And I've seen her change her mind when someone provides information to her that convinces her they're right.

I can count on her to be respectful even when she disagrees. I can count on her to tell me when she doesn't like something I've done or said. She's plainspoken, but friendly. She doesn't act like she thinks others owe her something.

What does your partner say and do that demonstrates character?
All of the above. She lives by her principles, which are well thought out values that have credibility in the world. She can maintain her position when she truly believes she's right, even when others try to get her to back down and win their approval. She's a nurse and on many occasions she's disagreed with a physician on their diagnosis or treatment of a patient. One time she disagreed with a group of doctors who insisted they were right and she was wrong. The only problem was that their disagreement was over a 24-year-old young man's diagnosis. No matter how much she was able to back up her opinion with fact they wouldn't listen. She was so distressed that their diagnosis would ruin this young man's life that she fought them on their position. When they still wouldn't listen she took the chance of presenting the case to the teaching expert that visited their hospital once a month to do teaching rounds. She was the first nurse in the hospital to ever present a case to teaching rounds, but she did it even though she was feeling intimidated by the doctors. The physicians could have

easily humiliated her and in the early stages of the conference it appeared that she would indeed be humiliated in grand style.

So she presented the case to the teaching physician in front of a room full of doctors – all of whom disagreed with her – and other health care professionals. The physician listened attentively and asked thoughtful questions. When she finished presenting the case and her distress over what she believed to be an incorrect diagnosis that would have a serious negative impact on the young man's life, several other physicians spoke up and said why she was wrong. After all, 12 other physicians had diagnosed him the same way. The visiting physician looked at her and apologetically shrugged his shoulders. And then he said he'd interview the patient, which he proceeded to do in front of the group.

As she watched the diagnostic interview she saw this visiting expert agree with her openly before the roomful of doctors. After an hour-long interview the verdict was clear. The visiting professor turned to her and said, "my dear, your are exactly right about the diagnosis and the physicians are wrong. You have saved this young man's life". He went on to teach about the fine points of the diagnosis and the treatment of the correct diagnosis. My partner was correct and she'd saved this young man from a lifetime of inappropriate treatment that would have ruined his life.

Not much in life takes more courage than this event. And I could tell you more stories of similar circumstances. I feel I can trust her with my life. If she believes in something and can back it up with fact, there's not much she won't do to convince others if the outcome may affect someone's life for better or worse.

What does your partner say and do that demonstrates integrity?
All of the above. There's not much else to be said. When she knows something to be true, even though her position may be unpopular with others, she'll stick with the position and do everything she can to show others the truth. The fact that she may feel somewhat anxious or put off about the way others treat her doesn't interfere with her doing what's right.

Benjamin's answer to question #5
My partner and I are very attracted to each other. We both light up when we see each other. Our attraction to each other has already increased over time and I expect it to keep getting better and better.

Part II

Sometimes Leaving Can Be Love

When the Best Thing to Do is to Leave

Couple #1's Decision

Gary and Susan came to the conclusion that they should divorce. Initially, Gary put up resistance in the form of making Susan's life a nightmare depriving her of enough money to pay the bills. Gradually, as Gary resolved his grief, he realized that he was harming himself and his children, as well as, Susan by behaving in such a way. Gradually he realized that, if he could let go of his resentment he had a real chance at real love. If he could grow, he could find a better marriage partner.

Divorce is never easy. Divorce always hurts. It is worth every ounce of strength and all of your energy to find the right marriage partner and prevent divorce. However, when you've already missed the boat, a dignified divorce can happen gracefully if you decide that's what you want. The need for everyone to win doesn't go away. It's basic human respect and you must do whatever you can to effect the least damage possible.

Mediators are available in many areas. Try to work out a separation agreement between you. Seek mediation if necessary. Go to the lawyer only when you have an agreed upon separation document. By doing so, you may be able to avoid an adversarial divorce entirely. Lawyers stand to gain the most with lots of conflict.

Unfortunately, not every partner is willing to separate and divorce. Whatever conflict or power struggles are going on in the marriage may escalate and intensify in the divorce. When this happens, please Don't lead someone to believe that you may tryagain later. Don't confuse the other person or your-self. Be clear about ending the relationship.

Don't be surprised if, even knowing that this is the wrong person to marry that you miss them. Don't be surprised that you'll have a period of grief. Let yourself grieve. Don't confuse grief with loving someone. It is possible to feel loving toward the wrong partner. Ending the relationship is still the right thing to do.

While you're grieving for what isn't to be, think back over your times together and your relation-ship and think about what worked and what didn't work. Be clear about that so you can move on and choose a better partner the next time. This ended relationship wasn't a total waste of time. It offered you an opportunity to practice relationship and marital skills. It gave you practice being a friend. This relationship gave you a chance to get to know yourself better. If you learn all you can, next time you'll have a better chance of finding the right per-son.

While you're grieving, do nice things for yourself. Take especially good care of yourself. Catch up on some of your other friendships. Update your look. Visit your family of origin and your friends and practice being yourself. Read some good books. Read *Perfect Partners™: Make Your Hopes and Dreams for a Great Marriage Come True*. Work through the workbook *Perfect Partners™: Find Your Perfect Partner Step-By-Step*.

Because of your own grief, you're children may experience your emotional absence. Be sure to involve your extended support group in your life protect yourself with legal advice and assistance –

the sooner the better. You may not be able to nego-tiate under some circumstances and an adversari-al divorce may be all you can achieve. The point is to take good care of yourself.

Rejection

When you end a relationship you have to deal with rejection. And rejection feels bad.

Think about this: When someone rejects you they help you notice that something about your rela-tionship isn't right. They help you end the wrong relationship. Notice those two words: Help you.

Rather than take the ending of a relationship per-sonally, take it as it is. Rejection plainly and sim-ply is the end to something that isn't working – and if you're the one being rejected – you just haven't noticed yet.

If you're on the receiving end of rejection – remem-ber that your partner is helping you recognize that something is wrong and helping you do what is best to do. Yes, you'll hurt. Yes, you'll be lonely for a little while. But you will live. You'll be far more okay than trying to live through a bad marriage. And best of all, you'll have the opportunity to find the right partner, now.

If you are doing the rejecting, be kind and friendly, but be clear. Set clear boundaries about this being the end of the relationship. It doesn't work to "let someone down easy." Be plainspoken and clear. and the lives of your children to minimize their fear and anxiety – to bridge the gap until you can be more fully available to them.

Make a new beginning.

List your favorite things to do for yourself. How do you pamper yourself? How do you take especially good care of yourself?

_____

_____

_____

_____

_____

_____

_____

_____

_____

_____

_____

_____

_____

_____

_____

_____

_____

_____

_____

_____

_____

_____

Write exactly what you will do to make a new beginning.

_____

_____

_____

_____

_____

_____

_____

_____

_____

_____

_____

_____

_____

_____

_____

_____

_____

_____

_____

_____

_____

_____

Name members of your support system – those you can turn to when you need an ear, or a shoulder, or some company.

_____

_____

_____

_____

_____

_____

_____

_____

_____

_____

_____

_____

_____

_____

_____

_____

_____

_____

_____

_____

_____

_____

Describe what problems and issues each of your children may have.

_____

_____

_____

_____

_____

_____

_____

_____

_____

_____

_____

_____

_____

_____

_____

_____

_____

_____

_____

_____

_____

Name each child's support system. Who and what can help you give emotional and physical support to your children?

_____

_____

_____

_____

_____

_____

_____

_____

_____

_____

_____

_____

_____

_____

_____

_____

_____

_____

_____

_____

_____

Finish Unfinished Business

If you are to offer yourself the best chance possible to find your perfect partner at some point in the future, you must finish the business of your marriage and any unfinished business from your past. The sooner you get started, the better.

One very helpful theoretical framework for working with couples having marital difficulties was developed by Murray Bowen, MD, of Georgetown University. His framework can help you finish past issues and ready yourself to function at a higher level in your next relationship. He and his followers say that problems in relationships originate from learning certain relationship styles in your family of origin. Relationship styles are imprinted on you before you even have language to describe what's happening. And they say that to treat relationship problems that you have as an adult you must return to your family of origin and work out the original conflicts. Without doing so you are doomed to repeat the dynamic over and over. We call the repetition of behavior patterns repetition compulsion.

In a simplified explanation of Bowen's theory: People have varying degrees of anxiety related to their level of fusion or differentiation. Fusion means having very little self, forcing you to borrow the identity of others (pseudo or false self) and differentiation meaning having a strong sense of self as differentiated from members of your family of origin and others. People use a variety of methods to alleviate their anxiety. They use relationship styles to manage their anxiety. The styles those who have a high to moderate level of fusion use to manage the anxiety in their relationships cause a multitude of problems. And those problems result in a need to return to the family of origin to address the real problem.

Treatment calls for a return to the family of origin in order to differentiate yourself from other family members. Essentially that means that you need to spend individual time with individual family members and learn to define yourself to them by verbalizing your opinions about topics and subject matters in a calm and friendly way. You practice inviting others to express their opinions without attack or defensiveness, allowing them to be themselves. You develop the skill of having your own opinion and allowing others to have their own opinions. You learn not to react emotionally to others behavior and opinions, but to use your intelligence to think for yourself. You learn to be present with your family of origin, without the emotional roller coaster ride.

As you practice this new way of relating to family members you differentiate a self, which is necessary for a great marriage. It's pretty easy to see why. You have to know yourself to know who your perfect partner is. You have to live your life on purpose to have a good life. You have to be the master of your behavior separate from your emotions. People with a high level of differentiation have more successful relationships and more successful lives.

Don't jump into your next relationship too soon. Finish grieving. Use your time and energy to work on yourself.

Part III

Have a Great Marriage

When You Know the Best for Everyone is to Stay

Couple #2's Decision

Anne Marie and Matthew agree that they belong together. They want to spend the rest of their lives together and feel certain they can resolve their past issues ridding their marriage of their ghosts. They have some work to do, but we feel certain that they can do very well and have a great marriage.

Please understand that unless you have what it takes to have a great marriage we believe that you owe it to yourself, your mate, and your children to leave and find your perfect partner. We recommend that you leave. We realize that some of you will have tremendous resistance to doing so. Only you can decide. But we encourage you to be clear about what you're choosing. You are settling for second best, which is usually taking the easy way out.

Remember the public's reaction to the book and movie, The Bridges of Madison County? What a moving story it was. Have you thought about why that story had such an impact on our emotions? We think it's because of the profound and universal choice of accepting second best and not rocking the boat or living your life to its highest potential. The vast majority of people choose what they believe is possible – second best. And that choice tears at their soul. When we saw that choice in living color, we cried – we sobbed.

And what about Princess Diana? Here was a young woman that touched our lives and our hearts. Why was it that so many people loved her and became intrigued by her life? Wasn't the pain she wore in front of her public our pain? Didn't it remind us of how much we want our marriages and romances to work out for our families and us?

Yes, if you can master relationship skills such that you can create a peaceful coexistence, you'll improve your family life. You will still deprive yourself of the energy – the synergy – created by marriage to your perfect partner. You'll probably fall short of the best that you can be.

Yes, your children will be better off in a household of low conflict – if you can master better relationship skills. But they will still have to choose sides every time they work on their own differentiation in regard to values. They will feel as though their loyalties are put to the test when they explore values and guiding principles. How do they choose between mom and dad? That's what it will feel like to them. Choosing between teachers' ideas isn't so bad, but mom and dad's? They will still have role models that settle for second best. Is that what you want for your children – to have second best? Children do what they see not what you say. They will still be exposed to lukewarm interactions, not the kind of energized and enthusiastic interactions that inspire.

If you've decided to stay even though your degree of matching on the 16 differences is below optimum, you must do everything possible to master relationship skills. You must become an expert at respectful conflict resolution, negotiation, and communication.

If you've decided to stay under these conditions – please stop and reconsider.

More hopefully, for those of you that have clearly found your perfect partner because you have a high degree of matching on the 16 differences that make a difference, but suffer from poor relationship skills – let's get to work and master a higher level – a more mature level of function.

Describe the strengths of your marriage. Include
information from the five crucial questions. At the
very minimum you'll be able to list a score of 130
or above on the 16 differences that make a difference.

_____

_____

_____

_____

_____

_____

_____

_____

_____

_____

_____

_____

_____

_____

_____

_____

_____

_____

_____

_____

Describe the weaknesses of your marriage. Include exactly what relationship skills you, as a couple, must master to give yourselves a great marriage.

_____

_____

_____

_____

_____

_____

_____

_____

_____

_____

_____

_____

_____

_____

_____

_____

_____

_____

_____

_____

Make a plan for improving your relationship skills and level of function. Include the resources you have that can help you achieve a higher level of function, such as books, professionals, tapes, etc. Remember that you can only change yourself, so focus on what each one of you can do to change yourselves for the better. Make a decision as to whether you think you and your mate can achieve what you want on your own or will you need professional help?

_____

_____

_____

_____

_____

_____

_____

_____

_____

_____

_____

_____

_____

_____

_____

_____

_____

Couple #2's Answers

The strengths of our marriage is how well we match on the 16 differences that make a difference. We'd match even better without the conflict we've had recently. We had four very good years and we still have good times. We think we can get that back again. We love each other and we have great kids. We want to spend the rest of our lives together.

The weaknesses of our marriage are poor relationship skills – particularly conflict resolution. We both have unfinished business that is affecting our marriage and we need to resolve that. We need to get back to having more fun with each other.

Our plan is to continue therapy and learn new conflict resolution skills. We can practice new skills in therapy and at home as we work out past issues. We're going to concentrate on defining our unfinished business clearly and determining what we can do about it. Then we're going to resolve it.

Our Comments

Anne Marie and Matthew are on the right track. The assessment of their strengths and weaknesses is accurate. They have what it takes to accomplish their plan. People are often surprised that finishing their unfinished business is easier than all of the things they do to avoid it. They should be in pretty good shape in another 10-12 weeks. They may need intermittent boosters from therapy as things go along, but they'll master the skills they need quickly.

Are You in a Long-term Relationship, but not Married?

If you're not married, get married. Notice that we said "great marriage" not "great live-in." The kind of relationship we are talking about includes marriage – the legal and/or religious kind. Which brings us to two topics of great importance for great marriages:

1. Great sex, and
2. Special boundaries: Ceremonies, rituals, and symbols.

Great Sex

Great sex is a component of every great marriage. Unfortunately, many people don't know how to have great sex.

Intimacy – the sharing of your real self, your private thoughts and feelings, with another person – is the emotional climate of a great marriage. The sexual relationship you have with your partner deepens the level of intimacy in your relationship; your sexual relationship enlarges intimacy to include physical intimacy with emotional and mental intimacy.

Research shows that intimacy – having someone you feel emotionally safe to confide in – saves lives.

There isn't anything much more special than the personal pleasure your partner can create for you and help you create for yourself than knowing how to pleasure you sexually. Providing and receiving sexual pleasure is extremely good and very special. Sexual intimacy is what separates this relationship from other good friendships. Sexual intimacy is what two adults experience in a great marriage.

As we said before, marriage is for adults. So we're talking about the kind of physical attraction and chemistry that two adults have for each other. This kind of adult attraction is the result of building intimacy, emotional safety, positive regard, and a history together. It is not the kind of flirtation that those looking for some company and affection display and not the kind of flirtation that turns out to be attention-getting rather than an adult sexual response.

Adult sexual response cannot be faked or taught. It happens to adults that have fully developed emotionally and physically.

Because sex is so private and such a personal activity it's hard to teach others, but not impossible. Unfortunately, few people have the opportunity to learn the particulars about great sex. Many men express confusion about female sexual response and many females express consternation over their man's lack of knowledge of how to pleasure their female partner. Many men don't realize that the majority of women need stimulation other than intercourse to have an orgasm.

Talking about sex is difficult between strangers and with those you don't trust, but relatively easy between friends that trust each other. Your perfect partner can talk to you about sex and sexual pleasure. They can guide you about what gives them pleasure and they want to know about what gives you pleasure. When you've gained the level of trust and companionship that perfect partners have, talking about sex loses its uncertainty.

Because great sex is so important and so little is written to advise us about what great sex is and how it happens, we've made the topic a priority in our book. If you'd like some guidance about great sex, if you want an example of great sex, read our chapter on great sex in our book *Perfect Partners™: Make Your Hopes and Dreams for a Great Marriage Come True* (Publication due in January 1998).

After several discussions about the importance of great sex and how important it was for us in our own marriage, we decided to include a personal example of great sex. Deciding to do so took time and careful handling of our sensitivity about our own privacy, but in the end we decided we had to suspend our egos and tell you what works. Too many people don't know and many patients of Carolyn's have benefited from learning what to do. One of Carolyn's young male patients expressed great relief to know what to do and for how long.

If you need personal guidance about having great sex, please turn to the chapter on great sex in our book. It has helped many people.

You deserve to have great sex. You deserve to have the benefits of great sex.

In the meantime, turn to the next exercise to evaluate your sexual relationship and how much you

know about your partner's and your own sexual
response.

Describe your partner

What does your partner like to have you do that gives him or her sexual pleasure? What activities help your partner have an orgasm?

_____

_____

_____

_____

_____

_____

_____

_____

_____

_____

_____

_____

_____

_____

_____

_____

_____

_____

_____

_____

_____

Describe yourself

What do you like your partner to do to give you sexual pleasure? What activities help you have an orgasm?

_____

_____

_____

_____

_____

_____

_____

_____

_____

_____

_____

_____

_____

_____

_____

_____

_____

_____

Benjamin's answer to questions about sexuality

What does your partner like you to do that gives him or her sexual pleasure? What activities help your partner have an orgasm?

My partner likes me to take some time to lay and talk with her about things for a few minutes. Usually we begin to kiss and hug and touch each other as we talk and laugh. After a short time – five to 15 or 20 minutes – I begin to touch her more and concentrate on her breasts and lightly brushing her clitoris. After two or three minutes I focus more intently on stimulating her nipples and clitoris. We both like her to have an orgasm first, before I let myself become more aroused. After about four or five minutes of stimulating her this way, we switch positions and she stimulates her clitoris exactly the way she likes, while I focus on increasing stimulation of her nipples and the muscles in her vagina. I can tell by the sounds she makes and the way that she moves just what she wants me to do and when. She usually has an orgasm five minutes or maybe a little longer after we switch positions and intensify the stimulation. Sometimes we vary the earlier stimulation with oral sex.

We had great sex right away because she wasn't afraid to tell me and show me what she wanted me to do. She also knew that the majority of women can't have an orgasm from intercourse so she isn't intimidated into the frustration of trying to become aroused enough by intercourse.

The best thing is that, by having her orgasm before we stimulate and arouse me, she can become re-aroused easily by intercourse and has multiple orgasms when we have intercourse. It is deeply

satisfying to her and to me. Our sexual relationship is amazingly satisfying.

**What do you like your partner to do to give you
sexual pleasure? What activities help you have
an orgasm?**
After my partner climaxes, I lay quietly with her for
a minute or two and then we shift our positions so
she can stimulate me. I like her to kiss me and
touch my penis. Sometimes she does oral sex on
me. I like to look at her body and do so arouses me
more. She isn't shy about letting me look, which I
like. These days I'm aroused pretty quickly and
when I have a good erection, we have intercourse
in two or three favorite positions. Intercourse
makes my partner have more orgasms. I take my
time and give her and myself pleasure for 10 or 15
minutes and then I have an orgasm. Both of us like
to lay quietly talking or watching TV or reading,
enjoying the way we feel for some time after we're
finished.

I feel free to tell my partner what I like because
she's so accepting and enjoys her body and my
body and sexual expression as much as I do.

Sex in my first marriage was a disaster because my
ex-wife would never tell me what she wanted and
she hated me to look at her. Her attitude about me
and about sex turned it into a chore and a seriously negative endeavor in our marriage.

What a relief and joy to have great sex.

Great sex is derived from and contributes to a great
marriage. Great sex is the icing on the cake.

A Word about Quickies

Because of our own experiences with quickies and many of Carolyn's patients' experiences, we want to tell you our thoughts about quickies.

After especially satisfying sex, one partner – usually the woman, but sometime the man – doesn't feel the desire to have sex as soon as his or her partner. His or her partner wants to make love, but he or she isn't up for the whole nine yards. When such a situation happens, it's nice when the partner that doesn't want to have sex will have some fun and have a quickie. Maybe you're sick of people for the moment or tired or just want to read. Providing the opportunity for your partner to have a quickie is perfect for both partners. One partner can satisfy himself or herself relatively quickly and the other partner can turn over and read or watch TV or otherwise vegetate without a great expenditure of time and energy. Quickies are perfectly acceptable for many people.

Let's be clear. Quickies are only good sometimes. Great sex includes the mutually satisfying form of making love. But quickies serve a perfectly normal purpose at times.

Boundaries

Most of you are already married. You'll still benefit from reading what we have to say about special boundaries. For those of you not yet married, great marriages deserve great beginnings. If you find yourself certain that you've found your perfect partner, it's time to plan what to do next. If you're already married and recommitted to your marriage, think about reaffirming your vows.

Here we'd like to give you some guidance about your options when you've found your perfect partner. We'll discuss the first task of marriage, boundaries, and special boundaries.

The First Task of Every Marriage

Judith Wallerstein, author of *The Good Marriage* (Houghton Mifflin, 1995), has been doing research on the effects of divorce on children for 25 years. Having determined that divorce wreaks havoc on the lives of children, Wallerstein decided that we have to get a better grip on having successful marriages. Recently she conducted research on 50 self-described, good marriages. In doing her research, she defined nine tasks that every marriage must master in order to have a good marriage. We want to tell you about the first task. For more complete information on all nine tasks read Wallerstein's book, *The Good Marriage*.

The first of those nine tasks is that the individuals in a new marriage – beginning when the relationship takes a turn toward marriage – must shift their primary loyalty from their family of origin to their partner and unite together as a couple and later a family. In order to do so you must have good couple boundaries. To have good couple boundaries you must begin by having good individual boundaries.

Personal Boundaries

Boundaries are the limits you will tolerate for your own and others' behavior. Having a strong sense of self, knowing how you think and feel, proactivity rather than reactivity, thinking for yourself, matching your behavior to your beliefs and values, acting with intention, liking yourself, and the behavior you'll accept from others – are the boundaries that define you. We've asked you to define who you are so you can be clear about your boundaries. The most successful people have strong, clear boundaries that neither allow unacceptable intrusiveness by others, nor isolation from others. People with strong and clear boundaries neither have to borrow a self from others nor feel a need to foist their identity on others. People with clear boundaries don't confuse others about what their boundaries are.

The most basic, fundamental element of great marriages is individuals with clear and strong boundaries. When two people with clear and strong boundaries match on those boundaries – the 16 differences that make a difference are types of boundaries – and they have strong boundaries about the other four questions, they have the ability to have good couple boundaries. It takes good couple boundaries to master the first task of marriage.

Couple Boundaries

When you become a couple and turn your intention toward marriage, the world must be informed of the birth of your new status and intention to commit to one another. This is another circumstance where you have to back up your words with action.

Because of boundary issues and legal issues, we believe that marriage is important. Living with someone just never has the same level of commitment and the benefits of a great marriage cannot happen without commitment and emotional safety. Living with someone cannot give you the same level of synergy that marriage gives you. We believe that marriage is a boundary – it's a special boundary that we'll talk more about in a moment.

The task of shifting your primary loyalty to you and your partner as a couple and the beginning of a new family requires setting boundaries from the point that you decide you'll marry. When you can be clear about this first boundary as a couple many other things about starting your lives together will clarify.

When we got married four years ago, we had to set boundaries as a couple. It didn't matter that we'd been married before. We had to master the first marital task, again, as does everyone who wants a great marriage.

First, we encountered family members that wanted to tell us how to have our wedding. Then we had other family members that wanted us to honeymoon at their house with them. Then we had family that wanted us to take annual vacations with the rest of the family. Other issues came up around how and where to live, how to act, how to parent, where to sit at ballgames. And on and on. It's pretty amazing how others want you to do and act as they believe proper and think it strange that you may have your own way – or never even consider that you may have your own ideas about what you intend to do. Frankly, the more insecure people are, the more they want to control others to make their lives more predictable.

When we first got together, Wes had never really heard the term boundaries used the way we're describing boundaries. In fact, boundaries – or a lack of them – are a big issue in his family of origin. But Wes is a quick study and he caught on fast. And he felt much better for it, too. In no time we were acting in our own best interest as a couple. It felt great.

Carolyn had already had plenty of practice both in her own life and as a therapist in setting limits and helping others to set limits.

Setting couple boundaries takes a unified couple. You will fail your partner if you fail to shift your primary loyalty to your partner and the two of you as a couple.

We handled each of these incidences with consistency and firm determination and eventually the fury died down. It flares up now and again, and we find ourselves taking a deep breath and setting limits again.

Setting limits and having clear boundaries empowers us to live our lives exactly the way we want to live our lives. We have control of our own lives. People that don't have control of their own lives are depressed, angry, and resentful. It doesn't occur to them that it's up to them to take control and set limits. Realizing that it's up to them is liberating and empowering.

One more thing. We've had people accuse each of us at various times of being controlling. The truth is, we are controlling over our own lives. We don't allow others to intrude unless we want them to. We speak up clearly for our needs to be met. We don't believe that it is harmful controlling in an attempt to get others to do only what we want, but it is the kind of effectiveness that mature individuals have in their lives. There's a difference between controlling others manipulatively and setting the kind of limits necessary to have your life effectively under control. It would be wise for those people to stop and consider why they have a need to get us to act just the way they want. Are those accusations that we're controlling – which most people don't want to be – attempts to manipulate by guilt?

The point is you must be prepared to listen to yourself. When you set limits and someone doesn't like the limit, they may try a variety of things to get their way. You must be prepared as an individual and as a couple to maintain your limits and your boundaries firmly and clearly. Don't allow yourselves to be pulled off center.

In our case, we just said over and over that we would handle our own wedding plans. Something about weddings brings out the craziness in every family. Everyone thinks they know best. Many family members feel the wedding belongs to them. As with advice about anything, we'd listen to others' opinions and then decide for ourselves what we intended to do. That was no small task at times. Have you ever seen grown adults manipulating, and insinuating, and contorting to get their way? The guilt trips can be amazing. Well they tried everything. But no one can control you unless you let them. We just held a steady course and had the wedding we wanted to have.

Have the wedding you want to have. It's your wedding. Start your marriage off right and set limits.

As for the honeymoon – we would never consider having our honeymoon with others. And they thought we were off our rockers. After all, we'd each been married before – what's the big deal? Well it is a big deal. We wanted to be alone. We wanted to follow our own schedule. We wanted to go somewhere different.

Have the honeymoon you want to have. It's your honeymoon. Begin your marriage right – set its tone.

The annual family vacation was a big issue. It took months to convince others we meant business and would take our vacations when and how and where we wanted. Of course others took it personally. They didn't consider that Carolyn spends her work time with unhappy couples and families and spending her vacation that way wouldn't be any vacation for her. They didn't consider that we wanted to go different places and see new things. They didn't consider that we have so much fun together that we don't need a huge crowd or that we might want to spend quality fun time with each other. They didn't consider that we wanted to do something different than they wanted to do. So we just stayed the course and finally the roar died down. The family has discovered that our having our vacation how and where and when we wanted didn't mean we didn't love them. It didn't mean that we never wanted to see them. They realize that we mean business and that we've managed to see them, at times, too.

Carolyn can remember how horrible starting her first marriage was when the relatives kept fighting about where they would stay during visits and how much they'd see of each family. She vowed that she'd never put that kind of pressure on her children and their families. Keeping that promise to herself in mind, Christmas at her house comes in the afternoon after the young families have had some private time together or after Christmas Eve and morning with their wives' families. It's begun a new tradition. By the time everyone gets to her house all the other families feel satisfied and no one has to hurry. It's worked out beautifully. And when our married children are in town for Christmas we share them with each other (the in-laws) and have us to each other's houses. Our tradition setting is a boundary.

Other common day-to-day boundaries include asking people to call before they drop by, answering the phone when you want rather than whenever it rings, or being able to excuse yourself from a phone call when you're finished talking. Asking people to call during certain times when a new baby comes home and only to come over when pre-arranged is a boundary. Of course, you'll want to extend the same courtesies to others. Honor your own and others' boundaries.

New couples and new families must forge and protect their own boundaries and traditions. Start at the very beginning to set limits and have clear boundaries.

Back your partner up – even if your mother is

pulling every trick in the book to get her way. We all loved our mothers first, but you must shift your primary loyalty to your new family. Remind your mother of how much she would have wanted that for herself. Gentle and friendly firmness will help others respect the boundaries that you set for yourselves. Your partner, your marriage, your new family come first.

Special Boundaries – Rituals, Ceremonies, and Symbols

It is ironic to us that, today, as we write to you about special boundaries, the world is watching the funeral of Princess Diana. Funerals serve a purpose. Their ritual and ceremony offer us an opportunity to make a transition in our lives.

Funerals are an example of special boundaries. It was a funeral that heightened Carolyn's awareness years ago of the importance of rituals, ceremonies, and symbols – all special boundaries. Carolyn believed, before the funeral of her young mother-in-law, the grandmother of her children, that funerals seemed a waste. It was in living through the grief of her mother-in-law's sudden death that Carolyn learned how important it is to say good-bye – how important it is to take a moment and have closure.

It is through rituals, ceremonies, and symbols that we communicate to each other the changes in our status in life. We celebrate a baby's birth with birthdays. We reaffirm our spiritual beliefs through christenings and religious holidays. We recognize growth, gaining maturity, and independence through graduations and certain religious ceremonies. We say good-bye at wakes and funerals and offer one another emotional support for our grief and loss.

And we celebrate the significant change in status of individuals when they vow to live together in marriage with weddings and receptions. It is at a wedding that a couple says to others that they have committed to each other and future children to live together as husband and wife. After the wedding, it is wedding rings that symbolize those vows. Rings help us communicate our wedded status to others, serving to lessen the complexities of relationships.

It is at our wedding that we demonstrate to others and help them recognize the change in our status to a new family unit. Weddings afford us an opportunity to set a new boundary. Rings assist in setting that boundary. Honeymoons, alone, set a boundary of privacy for the beginning of this new primary unit – a new family.

We believe in weddings and marriage. Great marriages start with the right partners, engagements, weddings, and honeymoons.

Name your personal boundaries.

_____

_____

_____

_____

_____

_____

_____

_____

_____

_____

_____

_____

_____

_____

_____

_____

_____

_____

_____

_____

_____

Have your partner name his or her personal boundaries.

Together, name the couple boundaries that you'd like to set for yourselves as you start your renewed life together. (Even if you've been married for a while, you're starting anew by reaffirming your commitment together. With newly resolved ambivalence about your marriage you can make a fresh beginning.)

_____

_____

_____

_____

_____

_____

_____

_____

_____

_____

_____

_____

_____

_____

_____

_____

_____

Benjamin's answer to question about boundaries

As I thought about the answer to this exercise I realized that the description of my beliefs and practices in regard to the sixteen differences are largely my boundaries. In living up to my values I place limits on myself and others in relation to what I believe and practice. I used to have difficulty setting limits with others and saying "no" to them when I didn't want to do something, but not anymore. I realize that it's up to me to make my life the way I want to live it so I speak right up.

I'm learning to go directly to the person with whom I have a beef rather than complaining to others. When others want to come and visit, I let them know right away what I will and will not be able to do with them.

I don't answer the phone when I'm busy or resting and I don't drop in on my friends and family without calling. I expect them to do the same.

My partner agrees that her beliefs and practice as described for the sixteen differences go a long way toward defining her boundaries. She's been practicing setting limits longer than I have and is better at it than I am sometimes. My partner helped me learn more about boundaries and limits and we've gotten very good at our couple boundaries.

My partner and I would like others to respect our privacy by calling before they come over and asking us our plans for holidays before including us in their plans. We'd like to have our own family traditions. We agree that we'll not make plans that involve the other partner without consulting them first. And we won't make plans for both of us unless we talk it over. We'll probably continue to largely discuss most daily tasks and activities together and agree on where to spend our time, energy, and money.

Initially I didn't want to wear a wedding ring. I didn't in my first marriage and I hadn't even really thought about it. But my partner wanted me to wear a ring. As she explained her reasons to me I agreed that I would wear a ring. We want to have a wedding celebration, but not at a church and a different place for a reception. My partner has the idea of having our wedding ceremony at a beautiful restaurant and holding the reception in the same place. And I like that idea so that's what we're planning. We'll invite around 75 people – a mixture of friends, coworkers, and family. We're going to have a buffet for appetizers and wine or beer or soft drinks. We want to have the wedding in the early afternoon. And we'll have a wedding cake. We've decided that we'll have some quiet music without dancing.

We want our children to stand up for us as witnesses. We want to make traditional vows.

We've decided where we want to have our honeymoon and are looking forward to having some fun in the sun.

In Conclusion

Choosing the right marriage partner is the most important decision you'll make in your life. A successful marriage is the foundation for all of the other successes in your life.

We hope the information we've given you in this workbook will have provided you meaningful guidance in your struggle to decide whether to stay or to leave.

For those of you that failed to determine that your partner is your perfect partner, we encourage you with all of our energy to keep looking. You can find the right person. Just use your determination and our ideas and you'll find your perfect partner. If you haven't already ready read our book, Perfect Partners™: Make Your Hopes and Dreams for a Great Marriage Come True or our first workbook Perfect Partners™: Find Your Perfect Partner Step-By-Step, please do. Our book describes our ideas about love and marriage most completely. Our first workbook is about finding the right person. Both will contribute to a more successful outcome the next time.

For those of you that have found your perfect partner we say congratulations on a job well done. Please accept our very best wishes for a lifetime of happiness. Welcome to an ever-growing group of individuals and couples unwilling to accept anything less than the best.

Perfect Partners™/SM

Books, Workbooks & Consultation

Order next page and send to or call:

BookMasters, Inc.
P.O. Box 388
Ashland, OH 44805
Book Order Telephone: 800/247-6553
Email Order: order@bookmasters.com
http://www.bookmasters.com

Visit Carolyn & Wes Huff at their website
http://www.perfectpartners.net

For Ordering Book & Workbooks - Please Send:

The Book – Perfect Partners™ Make Your
Hopes and Dreams for a Great Marriage
Come True (The full text from which the
workbooks were derived, including our
our personal example of great sex). $24.95
(Available 1st quarter of 1998)   _____

The Workbook – Perfect Partners™: Find
Your Perfect Partner Step-By-Step (For
singles that are looking for their perfect
partner) $18.95   _____

The Workbook – Perfect Partners™: When
You Think You've Found Your Perfect Partner
Step-By-Step (For singles that want to know
if they have found their perfect partner; the
sequel to the previous workbook) $18.95
*This workbook is $10.00 when you buy it
together with Find Your Perfect Partner
Step-By-Step   _____

The Workbook – Perfect Partners™: Should
You Stay or Should You Leave? Step-By-Step
(For married couples in a troubled marriage)
$18.95   _____
State Tax Ohio Residents add 6%   _____

Shipping & Handling

$0 – 30.00	$5.95
30.01 – 60.00	7.95
60.01 – 90.00	9.95
90.01 – 150.00	12.95
150.01 – 250.00	15.95
250.00 +	Please call

TOTAL   _____

-continued next page-

Please enclose check or money order
for total - or   ———————

Please charge total to my credit card
(VISA or MC)   ———————

Account # _____ Exp. Date _____

Signature _____

To: Name _____
     Address_____
     City, State, Zip_____

_____

Phone & best time to call _____

_____

*Please see next page for ordering
phone consultation.

To Order Phone Consultation

Please use this form by mail to:

Perfect PartnersTM/SM
EMPOWERMENT SOLUTIONS INC.
550 M Ritchie Highway
Suite 142
Severna Park, MD 21146

or call (410) 647-6745 and leave a message to
arrange one hour of phone consultation for
help with personalizing the Perfect
PartnersTM/SM process. $250.00. We will
return your call to arrange a time conve-
nient to your schedule.

You will receive a free Perfect PartnersTM/SM book
or workbook of your choice when ordering
phone consultation. We will mail your
choice to you priority mail prior to our
phone consultation.

Name: _____

Address: _____

_____

Phone: _____

Best time to call: _____

_____

Name of free book choice: _____

_____

If paying by check or money order, please enclose
with this order form.
If paying by credit card (MC, VISA), we will bill
you at the time your appointment is
arranged.